GANDHI *for* KIDS

HIS LIFE AND IDEAS, WITH 21 ACTIVITIES

ELLEN MAHONEY

CHICAGO
REVIEW
PRESS

Published by Chicago Review Press Incorporated
814 North Franklin Street
Chicago, Illinois 60610
ISBN 978-1-61373-122-2

Library of Congress Cataloging-in-Publication Data
Names: Mahoney, Ellen Voelckers, author.
Title: Gandhi for kids : his life and ideas, with 21 activities / Ellen
  Mahoney.
Description: Chicago, Illinois : Chicago Review Press, 2016. | Series: For
  kids series | Includes bibliographical references and index.
Identifiers: LCCN 2015050677 | ISBN 9781613731222 (paperback) | ISBN
  9781613731253 (epub) | ISBN 9781613731239 (kindle)
Subjects: LCSH: Gandhi, Mahatma, 1869–1948—Juvenile literature. | Gandhi,
  Mahatma, 1869–1948—Study and teaching—Activity programs—Juvenile
  literature. | India—History—Study and teaching—Activity
  programs—Juvenile literature. | Statesmen—India—Biography—Juvenile
  literature. | Nationalists—India—Biography—Juvenile literature. |
  Nonviolence—India—History—20th century—Juvenile literature. |
  India—History—Autonomy and independence movements—Juvenile literature.
  | India—Politics and government—1919–1947—Juvenile literature. |
  Creative activities and seat work. | BISAC: JUVENILE NONFICTION /
  Biography & Autobiography / Social Activists. | JUVENILE NONFICTION /
  Biography & Autobiography / Historical. | JUVENILE NONFICTION /
  History / Asia.
Classification: LCC DS481.G3 M265 2016 | DDC 954.03/5092—dc23 LC
record available at http://lccn.loc.gov/2015050677

Cover design: Monica Baziuk
Cover images: (front cover, top row, from left) henna paisley illustration, Shutterstock,
  blue67design; map of India, Shutterstock, boreala; Hindu goddess Lakshmi, Shutterstock,
  Malgorzata Kistryn; Mahatma Gandhi, © Hulton-Deutsch Collection/CORBIS; spinning
  wheel illustration, Wikimedia Commons; (front cover, bottom row, from left) Gandhi as
  a lawyer, Wikimedia Commons; Gandhi at Sevagram Ashram, courtesy of Arun Gandhi;
  vegetables, author's collection; Aung San Suu Kyi, Wikimedia Commons, Creative
  Commons, Claude TRUONG-NGOC; (back cover, clockwise from top left) Gandhi with
  his brother Laxmidas, courtesy of Gandhi Heritage Portal; women with cow, courtesy
  of Himalayan Academy; henna paisley illustration, Shutterstock, blue67design; Ganesha,
  author's collection.
Interior design: Sarah Olson
Interior illustrations: James Spence

Printed in the United States of America
5 4 3 2 1

CONTENTS

NOTE TO READERS

The story of Gandhi takes you into the enchanting and unique worlds of India, South Africa, and England, where different cultures and languages come to life. You'll read about Gandhi's early life in India and glimpse the colorful festivals, animals, and foods that were integral parts of his life. From India, you'll travel with Gandhi to England and South Africa to learn about these countries.

Throughout Gandhi's life he spoke different languages to communicate with his family members, friends, teachers, employers, clients, political leaders, activists, and followers. He believed that knowing different languages helped him understand the world around him. Gandhi grew up in the state of Gujarat, India. He first learned and spoke Gujarati, which he favored as his dominant language. Gandhi also learned English as a child in British-ruled India, and he was versed in Indian languages such as Sanskrit and Hindi. To help you learn about and pronounce many of the different words and names throughout this book, a glossary and pronunciation guide are included in the back.

TIME LINE

1869 Mohandas Karamchand Gandhi is born on October 2 in Porbandar, India, in the state of Gujarat

1883 At 13 years old, Mohandas marries Kastur Kapadia in an arranged marriage

1888 Gandhi travels to England to study law; his first son Harilal is born

1891 Gandhi returns to India after earning his law degree

1893 Gandhi travels to Durban, South Africa, to work as a lawyer; he is thrown off a train for refusing to move from his paid first-class seat to a third-class seat

1894 Gandhi creates the Natal Indian Congress to fight discrimination against Indians

1896 Gandhi travels to India to bring his family to live with him in South Africa

1897 Gandhi is beaten by a mob of white settlers in Durban for his pro-Indian reform efforts

1899 Gandhi organizes the Natal Indian Ambulance Corps for the British during the Second Boer War

1904 Gandhi establishes the Phoenix Settlement near Durban, which is a communal ashram devoted to vegetarianism, spirituality, and sustainable farming practices

1906 Gandhi organizes a second ambulance corps during the Zulu Rebellion

1907 Gandhi organizes his first peaceful, nonviolent Satyagraha campaign to protest a law designed to register and fingerprint Asians

1908 Gandhi is imprisoned in a Johannesburg jail for instigating Satyagraha

1910 Gandhi establishes the Tolstoy Farm near Johannesburg

1913 Gandhi organizes a nonviolent march through the Natal and Transvaal regions

1914 Gandhi helps pass the Indian Relief Act of 1914

1914 Gandhi leaves South Africa and lives in England for five months

1914 World War I begins

1915 Gandhi returns to India and is welcomed as a hero

1917 Gandhi establishes the Sabarmati Ashram in Ahmedabad, Gujarat; he helps the farmers of Champaran

1918 World War I ends

1919 Gandhi helps organize protests against the Rowlatt Act, legislation aimed to suppress Indian rights

1919 The Jallianwala Bagh Massacre

1920 Gandhi begins his noncooperation movement; he organizes a boycott of British goods and encourages people to spin cotton and make their own clothes

1922   Chauri Chaura killings

1922   Gandhi is sentenced to six years in the Yerwada Central Jail in Pune, India

1927   The first edition of Gandhi's autobiography, *The Story of My Experiments with Truth*, is published; the second edition is published two years later

1930   From the Sabarmati Ashram, Gandhi sets out on the historic Salt March

1932   Imprisoned again in the Yerwada jail, Gandhi begins his historic fast on behalf of the untouchables

1939   World War II begins

1942   Gandhi helps launch the "Quit India" movement, demanding India's independence from British rule

1942   Gandhi and Kasturba are imprisoned at Aga Khan Palace in Pune, India

1943   Gandhi fasts 21 days to protest violence in India

1944   Kasturba dies

1945   World War II ends

1947   India gains independence from British rule and is separated into India and Pakistan

1948   Gandhi, 78 years old, is assassinated by a Hindu nationalist on January 30

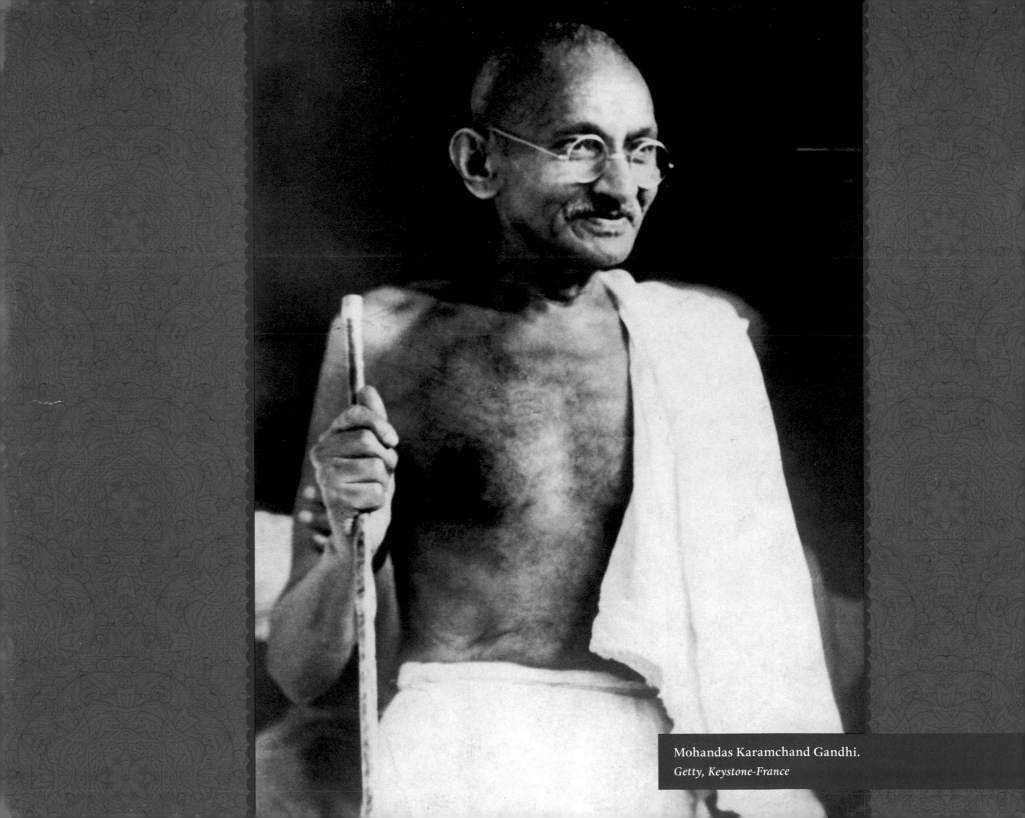

Mohandas Karamchand Gandhi.
Getty, Keystone-France

INTRODUCTION
MOHANDAS GANDHI

Generations to come, it may well be, will scarce believe that such a one as this ever in flesh and blood walked upon this Earth. —Albert Einstein

With his wire-rimmed glasses, homespun clothes, and walking stick, Gandhi is an unforgettable symbol of nonviolence, freedom, and peace for our world. Gandhi was a great leader of the 20th century who worked tirelessly and courageously to help India achieve its hard-won independence from England.

From childhood on, Gandhi led an extraordinary life with many fascinating twists and turns. He was a world traveler who lived in India, England, and South Africa. Traveling gave him wonderful opportunities to discover new lands and to observe how a wide variety of people did or did not get along.

His personal life had joys and sorrows. Gandhi was Hindu, and teenage marriages arranged by parents were traditional when he was young. He was married at the age of 13 to a hometown girl named Kastur, who was also his age. As was customary, Kastur's name became "Kasturbai" once she was married, and "Kasturba" when she was older and the matriarch of their family. Early in their marriage, the couple had a baby who died shortly after birth. Later in life, Gandhi and Kasturba raised four sons, named Harilal, Manilal, Ramdas, and Devdas.

Gandhi was often called "**Bapu**," which means "Father." In midlife, Gandhi was called "Mahatma," which means

"Great Soul." However, Gandhi was not comfortable being called Mahatma. He preferred to be seen as a role model striving to make a positive difference in the world. He hoped people would follow in his footsteps.

Gandhi was a high-energy person who related to a wide range of people. Many individuals, young and old, were drawn to him. Gandhi had admirable qualities, but he also admitted to having flaws and making mistakes. In his autobiography, *The Story of My Experiments with Truth*, Gandhi wrote about his life and work, as well as the hard times he experienced with the people closest to him. He could be stern and stubborn, as well as short tempered and contradictory. He could also be lenient, accepting, lighthearted, and loving. He was frequently away from home for work, and Kasturba was often in charge of raising their children.

A strict vegetarian, Gandhi was constantly searching for simple, hearty, meat-free foods. He was very interested in health and hygiene, and he even wrote a book titled *Key to Health*. In his youth Gandhi dreamed of becoming a doctor, but his father wanted him to become a lawyer. The skills he learned as a lawyer were beneficial on his path to becoming a leader. In a vibrant journey of self-transformation, Gandhi went from being a shy and tongue-tied young lawyer to standing before thousands of people and delivering powerful speeches.

Gandhi worked hard for Indian rights in both India and South Africa. Although he sought to bring about harmony, much of his life was enveloped in conflict and violence. He was harassed, humiliated, beaten, imprisoned, and eventually assassinated. He experienced war firsthand. In South Africa he lived through the Second Boer War and the Zulu Rebellion. In England and India, he lived through World War I and World War II. But Gandhi believed there was a better, less violent way to live. He helped bring about change through his speaking, writing, marches, boycotts, fasts, and protests against injustice, which often landed him in jail. Gandhi spent a sum total of nearly six years in jail.

Gandhi saw goodness in people and accepted many different religions beyond his Hindu faith. He believed in truth, justice, civil rights, and freedom, and he always sought to promote important ideals: be kind to others, seek truth, respect differences, practice nonviolence, and know change is possible. In India Gandhi is known as Father of the Nation, and his inspiring message of nonviolence lives on.

EARLY YEARS BY THE SEA

If we could change ourselves, the tendencies in the world would also change. As a man changes his own nature, so does the attitude of the world change towards him. —M. K. Gandhi

When Mohandas Karamchand Gandhi was born on October 2, 1869, in the small coastal town of Porbandar, India, his world was already changing. By his birthday, the torrential rains and high winds brought on by the region's monsoon season had passed, and drier, more comfortable winter days were on the way.

Porbandar was a seaport located in the large state of Gujarat in northwest India. Situated on the shores of the Arabian Sea in the ear-shaped Kathiawar Peninsula, Porbandar overlooked an expansive blue ocean framed by long stretches of white sandy beaches. It offered young Mohandas an exciting

place to live during his early childhood. Small fishing boats and large ships would come and go, and townsfolk could fish or swim in the ocean or fly kites and walk along the beach. As waves continually crashed against the shoreline, the port was often highlighted by beautiful rainbows, colorful sunsets, or dramatic lightning storms.

As a boy, Mohandas was surrounded by wildlife. Cows, horses, goats, cats, and dogs roamed the streets of Porbandar, and it was common to see oxen pulling passengers or cargo in two-wheeled or four-wheeled bullock carts. A wide range of colorful birds such as pink flamingos, great white pelicans, egrets, and herons could be seen flying about, perched in trees, or standing on beaches or in marshes. In the distant forests and plains of Gujarat, lions, leopards, and deer roamed their natural habitats.

Fishing was an important industry in Porbandar, and fishermen would take out their wooden boats and cast wide nets to catch shrimp, tuna, eel, squid, and catfish. The tangy smell of fish drying in the salty ocean breeze was a familiar scent around town. Porbandar was also a hub for trade with Africa and the Middle East, and large ships were often seen transporting products such as tobacco, timber, and cotton.

Gujarat was rich in the mineral limestone, and a thick limestone wall had been built near the water to protect the city from ocean storms and high waves. As it aged, the limestone wall eventually hardened and turned to a yellow-white color.

When the sun reflected off the white wall, it was a dazzling landmark for incoming sailors who could easily spot it. Porbandar was sometimes called "The White City" because of the wall's bright white appearance.

A BUSY HOME

Mohandas was born in a large three-story house in the heart of Porbandar, not far from the sea. Like most structures of the region, this building was constructed of limestone. Homes in the neighborhood were built close to one another with tight alleyways between them. Mohandas's neighborhood had narrow lanes that were lined with temples, shops, street vendors, and bustling bazaars.

The extended Gandhi family lived in this home for nearly a century before Mohandas was

(*below*) Mohandas when he was about seven years old.
Wikimedia Commons

(*right*) An early painting of Port Porbandar.
The British Library WD 4414 f.8v

born. He lived with his parents, a sister, and two brothers on the first floor, and his extended family of stepsiblings, cousins, aunts, uncles, and grandparents resided on the two upper floors. It was common for extended Indian families to all live under one roof in this way.

Wood-framed windows and a large door and veranda welcomed visitors to their box-shaped house. For decoration, intricate floral patterns adorned many walls and doorways. There were not many windows throughout the home, and because the sparsely furnished rooms tended to be dark, Mohandas's family relied on oil lamps for light and warmth. A large balcony on the upper floor provided sunshine and fresh air, and family members often enjoyed spending time there.

Freshwater was a precious commodity in Porbandar. Drinking water could taste salty, so the Gandhi family devised a way to obtain freshwater. Before the monsoon season, the flat roof of their three-story home was cleaned so it could catch rainwater. The rainwater was then funneled down through a pipe and stored in a large underground tank built below Mohandas's house.

Mohandas's home also had a small kitchen, where aromatic vegetarian dishes such as lentils with flatbread were prepared. Foods were cooked and water was heated on a stove fueled by firewood or cow dung patties. When ignited, the flat, round cow dung patties provided consistent heat for cooking.

A special family *puja* room was a sacred and serene area of the home used for prayer, worship,

Gandhi's home in Porbandar.
Courtesy of Gandhi Heritage Portal

and **meditation**. Mohandas's family members were Hindus and practiced the religion of **Hinduism**.

A CLOSE-KNIT FAMILY

Although Mohandas's father's name was Karamchand, friends and family fondly called him Kaba. For many years, Kaba experienced heartache. He had already been married three times when he

Hinduism

Hinduism is the most popular religion in India, and there are nearly one billion followers worldwide today. Hinduism is one of the three largest religions in the world along with **Christianity** and **Islam**. Many historians view Hinduism, which originated in India, as one of the oldest religions on Earth. Its followers are called Hindus, and there is no single founder or prophet.

Hinduism is a unique religion with a wide variety of deities, rituals, traditions, and celebrations. It is often regarded as a way of life that influences followers' everyday thoughts, feelings, and behaviors. Hindus accept different faiths as valid and believe that there are many paths to God, as expressed in the saying, "Truth is one, paths are many."

At the core of Hinduism is the worship of a Supreme Being. Hindus also worship many **deities**, which may take on human or animal features. Some of the most popular Hindu deities include **Rama** (an **avatar**, or human incarnation, of Vishnu), **Ganesha** (the elephant deity), **Krishna** (the blue-skinned deity), and **Lakshmi** (the goddess of good fortune).

Hinduism has four major denominations including Shaivism, which honors the deity Shiva as God; **Vaishnavism**, which honors **Vishnu** as God; Shaktism, which honors the Divine Mother as God; and Smartism, which honors many deities. Gandhi's family belonged to the Vaishnavism denomination and worshipped Vishnu and his divine avatars, Krishna and Rama.

The **Vedas** are sacred Hindu texts and shed light on four basic principles: **karma** (the consequences of one's positive or negative actions), **samsara** (the cycle of birth, life, death, and rebirth; **reincarnation**), all-pervasive divinity (the belief that God is everywhere, in everyone and everything), and **dharma** (the act of leading a righteous and compassionate life).

The Hindu goddess Lakshmi.
Shutterstock, Malgorzata Kistryn

married 13-year-old Putlibai in 1857. Two of Kaba's former wives had died, and he had two daughters from these previous marriages. His third wife was unable to bear children, which was difficult for the couple, and this marriage had also ended.

When Putlibai married Kaba, it was her first and only marriage, and she eventually gave birth to a daughter, Raliatbehn, and three sons: Laxmidas, Karsandas, and Mohandas, who was nicknamed "Moniya."

Raliatbehn, the eldest, often cared for young Moniya, as did his aunts, cousins, and a beloved nanny, Rambha. The entire family enjoyed Moniya's inquisitive nature, and Raliatbehn spent a great deal of time outdoors with her baby brother, as he loved to see the many animals around town.

Although Porbandar was a picturesque place to live, the town sometimes bothered Mohandas as he grew older. Hard-nosed, rum-drinking sailors with salty language and bravado frequented the seaport, and ancient tales of seafaring pirates abounded. In his autobiography, *The Story of My Experiments with Truth*, Gandhi admitted he was shy as a boy and frightened by many things, including thieves, ghosts, snakes, spiders, and even the dark. He often sought refuge in the safety of his home. Realizing Mohandas was struggling with many fears, Rambha encouraged him to repeat the word *"Ramanama"* over and over again for comfort and strength. "Ramanama" means the "name of Rama."

DEVOTED PARENTS

Kaba and Putlibai were hardworking individuals and had an important influence on Mohandas's entire life. Mohandas respected and admired his father but regarded him as somewhat stern. In his

Ganesha

Ganesha, the beloved elephant-headed god, is one of the most popular Hindu deities. Ganesha is the remover of obstacles in one's life, the destroyer of selfishness, vanity, and pride, and the reminder of life's abundance and joy.

Ganesha is depicted in different ways and often has four arms, two legs, and a round belly. In his hands he holds various symbolic objects,

such as a lotus flower for enlightenment, a small ax to sever negativity, and a plate of sweet dumplings to symbolize the rewards of a good life. Ganesha also holds up a right hand with his palm facing forward as a blessing of protection for all who view him. A small mouse sits beside Ganesha as a reminder that one's ego can nibble away at happiness and success in life.

Ganesha.
Author's collection

5

Create a Toran

In India, torans are used to adorn doorways, especially for Hindu festivals and weddings. Also called bandanwaars, these auspicious and welcoming door hangings are made with a variety of materials, such as leaves, flowers, fabric, beads, and metals. Torans often honor Lakshmi, the goddess of wealth and prosperity, and are symbols of love, happiness, and positive energy. Make your own toran with a festive design of mango leaves and marigolds.

YOU'LL NEED

* Printer paper
* Pencil
* Scissors
* 4 sheets of green construction paper
* Dark green colored pencil
* 1 sheet of yellow construction paper
* Dark orange colored pencil
* Paper punch
* Twine, 42-inch (107-cm) length
* Twine, 16 4-inch (10.2-cm) pieces

1. Use printer paper to trace the mango leaf and marigold flower patterns on this page, and cut each out.

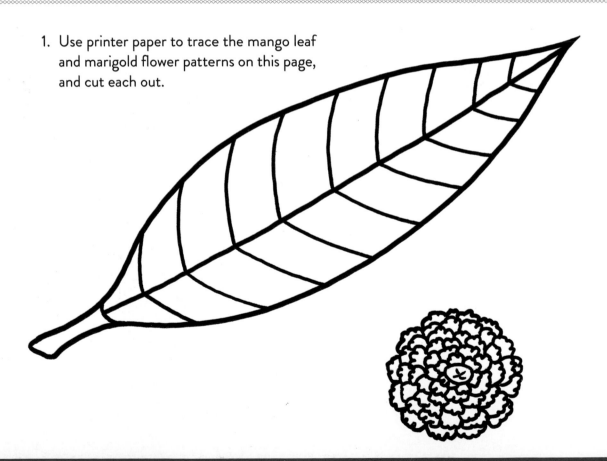

2. Use the leaf pattern you made in step 1 to draw and cut out 16 leaves on the green paper. Next, draw in the veins of each leaf with a dark green colored pencil.

3. Use the flower pattern you made in step 1 to draw and cut out 16 marigolds on yellow paper. Next, draw in flower petals on each flower with a dark orange colored pencil.

4. Place the flowers over the leaves at the top of the leaves, and use a paper punch to make a single hole in each of the 16 leaf and flower sets.

5. Use the 16 4-inch (10.2-cm) pieces of twine to tie the leaf and flower sets to the 42-inch length of twine.

6. Make a small loop at each end of your toran so you can hang it in a doorway.

(*left*) Gandhi's father, Karamchand Gandhi.
Courtesy of Gandhi Heritage Portal

(*right*) Gandhi's mother, Putlibai Gandhi.
Courtesy of Gandhi Heritage Portal

with individuals from diverse backgrounds. He also watched his father help his mother around the house with chores such as cutting vegetables or washing clothes. These insights played a key role in the young boy's future as a husband, father, and leader.

Mohandas had a close and caring relationship with his mother, and they seemed to have a lot in common. Putlibai was highly regarded in the community for her intellect and thoughtfulness. She took Mohandas and her other children along when she cared for others who needed medical attention. His mother's generosity helped him learn about being kind to others. She was also known for keeping a cool head. Once when a deadly scorpion came near her, she calmly picked it up and tossed it out the window.

Mohandas's mother belonged to the Pranami Vaishnava faith, which was a sect of Hinduism that included elements of Islam. She also grew up honoring the ancient traditions of **Jainism**, a religion that focused on vegetarianism, compassion, fasting, and tolerance. Putlibai had deep religious feelings but did not insist that others follow her beliefs or traditions. However, she did cultivate Mohandas's curiosity about religion, spirituality, and faith. She also planted many seeds in his mind about how to conduct one's life with integrity.

Mohandas's childhood was busy and filled with love. He grew up enjoying many Hindu holidays and festivals, such as **Diwali**, the Festival of Lights, which represents the start of the Hindu New Year. Diwali lasts five days and celebrates light over darkness and goodness over evil.

autobiography, Gandhi later wrote, "My father was a lover of his clan, truthful, brave and generous, but short-tempered." Kaba worked as a prominent Porbandar official called a *diwan* and was regarded as a man of high moral standing. When Mohandas would walk around Porbandar with his father, townsfolk would sometimes give him coins, sweets, and flatbreads out of respect.

Kaba enjoyed talking with many people from different religions and backgrounds, and he was very open to hearing others' points of view. As a boy, Mohandas observed how his father interacted

SPECIAL FAMILY TRADITIONS

Like many Hindus, the Gandhi family practiced vegetarianism; most family members did not eat meat. Putlibai also taught Mohandas about the practice of fasting, which is the intentional act of not eating foods for personal or religious reasons. The term *breakfast* refers to the breaking of one's fast after a night of sleep. At times Putlibai's fasting upset Mohandas. In his autobiography, he wrote about his mother's strict fasting during Chaturmas, a holy period that lasted four months from July to October and coincided with the rainy monsoon season.

To keep two or three consecutive fasts was nothing to her. Living on one meal a day during Chaturmas was a habit with her. Not content with that, she fasted every alternate day during one Chaturmas. During another Chaturmas she vowed not to have food without seeing the sun. We children on those days would stand, staring at the sky, waiting to announce the appearance of the sun to our mother. Everyone knows that at the height of the rainy season the sun often does not condescend to show his face. And I remember days when, at his sudden appearance, we would rush and announce it to her. She would run out to see with her own eyes, but by that time the fugitive sun would be gone, thus depriving her of her meal. "That does not matter," she would say cheerfully, "God did not want me to eat today." And then she would return to her round of duties.

Mohandas and his extended family members were part of an ancient Indian system of social classes. Often called castes, these self-governing classes were developed for social stability and a sense of community; members shared similar occupations and typically married within the

The Sacred Cow

In Hinduism the cow is revered and respected as a cherished symbol of life, abundance, strength, and the Earth. Hindus do not worship the cow as a deity, but rather the cow is an adored and protected animal that should never be injured or killed. Many Hindus are vegetarians and most

do not eat beef, but cows do provide Indian families with milk and cream, used to make ice cream, custard, yogurt, soft cheese, and ghee, which is a special clarified butter used in many foods. Cows often roam freely in the streets of India, and during special Indian festivals such as Diwali, cows are washed and decorated with garlands, paint, and ornaments; they are fed special sweets and paraded through towns.

Cows are sacred in Hinduism.
Courtesy of Himalayan Academy

Make Diya Candleholders

Diyas are traditional Indian lamps used for special occasions such as Diwali. These small, cup-shaped oil lamps are made of baked clay and typically use a cotton wick placed in the lamp's oil. You can make decorative diyas out of salt dough and use tea lights.

ADULT SUPERVISION REQUIRED

YOU'LL NEED

* Flour, 1 cup
* Salt, ½ cup
* Mixing bowl
* Water, ½ cup
* Fork
* Foil
* Cookie sheet
* Tea light
* Spatula
* Acrylic paints
* Paintbrush
* Craft glue
* Glitter and sequins
* Felt (optional)

1. Stir together the flour and salt in the mixing bowl. Slowly add water and mix all ingredients with a fork until the dough thickens.

2. Shape the dough into a small ball with your hands and then halve.

3. Place the two halves of the dough on a foil-covered cookie sheet. Shape and flatten each one into a round form with slightly dampened fingers.

4. Gently push a tea light into the center of each dough mound to form a groove for the candle.

Remove the tea light so you can widen the groove and smooth the clay. You can use a fork to make decorative ridges on the outside of the diyas.

5. Bake diyas (without tea lights) at 200 degrees Fahrenheit for three hours. Check them about every hour for doneness; they should slowly harden as they bake.

6. After baking, remove the diyas from the oven. Let them cool and harden for two days. Use the spatula to loosen the diyas from the cookie sheet. The top and bottom should dry completely.

7. Once the diyas have hardened, decorate them with paint, glitter, and sequins.

8. Place a tea light in the center of your finished diya. Remember—never leave a lit candle unattended.

group. The system was based on four main groups, called *varnas*, which included Brahmins (priests), Kshatriyas (kings and warriors), Vaishyas (traders, artisans, and farmers), and Shudras (peasants and laborers).

Mohandas's family belonged to a subcaste called Modh Bania of the larger Vaishya caste, and this was an important part of their lives and place in their community. The word *Modh* indicates the Gujarat region, and the word *Bania* means "trader."

A group known as "untouchables" existed as a community outside the caste system. These individuals were responsible for the most unclean work in the community, such as sanitation and cremation. As an adult, Gandhi believed untouchables were treated unfairly and preferred to call them Harijan, which means "children of God."

BETROTHED AT SEVEN

The betrothal and marriage between a boy and girl of the same religion and caste have been a tradition in Indian culture for centuries. It was a common practice when Mohandas was a boy. A betrothal is a formal agreement to marry someone else and is arranged by the parents of the bride and groom.

By the time Mohandas was seven years old, he had already been betrothed three times, but two of the girls had died. In 1876, seven-year-old Kastur Kapadia, a neighborhood girl, was chosen to be Mohandas's future bride. On a specially chosen day, Mohandas's father, Kaba Gandhi, visited Kastur's parents and asked if their daughter could marry his youngest son. The offer was accepted, and a decorative plate filled with fruits and flowers was placed on Kastur's head. A Hindu priest then gave his blessing to affirm the betrothal. After the engagement ceremony, guests enjoyed eating traditional Indian sweets and cookies.

Young Mohandas did not attend this engagement ceremony, and the newly betrothed couple would not marry for another seven years, when they were both 13 years old. But big changes awaited Mohandas in the months ahead. Kaba Gandhi had taken a new position as a diwan in the distant city of Rajkot. Everyone in the family was preparing to move inland, miles away from Porbandar and a long trek from the Arabian Sea. The years ahead would lead Mohandas to a whole new city, new country, and new way of life.

Bake Nan Khatai Cookies

Nan Khatai cookies are buttery, biscuit-like cookies that are very popular in India and fun to bake.

ADULT SUPERVISION REQUIRED

YOU'LL NEED

* Spoon (or spatula)
* Ghee, ½ cup (ghee is clarified butter; you can substitute unsalted butter)
* Powdered sugar, ½ cup
* 2 mixing bowls
* Water, ½ teaspoon
* Flour, 1 cup
* Cardamom powder, ¼ teaspoon
* Nutmeg, ¼ teaspoon
* Baking powder, ¼ teaspoon
* Salt, ⅛ teaspoon
* Plastic wrap
* Butter knife
* Pistachio nuts, halved
* Foil
* Cookie sheet
* Oven mitts

1. Use a spoon to mix the ghee (at room temperature) with the powdered sugar in a mixing bowl. Add ½ teaspoon water to moisten.

2. In the second mixing bowl, combine the flour with the spices, baking powder, and salt. Mix until combined.

3. Add the flour mixture to the ghee mixture a little at a time. Mix in well until a soft dough forms. Use your hands to knead the mixture into a ball.

4. Wrap the dough ball in plastic wrap and let it sit for 20 minutes.

5. Unwrap the dough and knead again. Now divide the dough into 12 equally sized round cookies. Use the butter knife to make an X in each cookie and add a halved pistachio nut in the center.

6. Place each cookie on a foil-covered cookie sheet and bake on center rack at 300 degrees Fahrenheit for 25 to 30 minutes. Cookies should look more white than brown when done.

7. Carefully remove the cookie sheet from the oven with oven mitts and let the cookies cool completely on the sheet.

Gandhi's new home in Rajkot.
Courtesy Gandhi Heritage Portal

NEW HORIZONS

If a man does not keep pace with his companions, perhaps it is because he hears a different drummer. Let him step to the music which he hears, however measured or far away. —Henry David Thoreau

To move to their new home, Putlibai, Kaba, and the four Gandhi children traveled inland nearly 90 miles, heading due east and then north to Rajkot, located on the banks of the Aji and Nyari Rivers. It was a long, five-day journey by ox-drawn carts. Rajkot was a drier, hotter, and more urban area than Porbandar. But like Porbandar, it had rainy monsoon months that would sometimes cause the nearby rivers to overflow. Still, Rajkot was a whole different world from the breezy coastal town of Porbandar.

LIVING IN RAJKOT

There were many adjustments accompanying the move, including living in a new home and attending a new school. It would be the first time Mohandas attended a formal British-run school, and he began learning English, which was very different from his native **Gujarati** language. Schoolwork could be challenging for him—he found multiplication tables difficult to memorize and reading wasn't easy for him. In his autobiography Gandhi wrote, "There is hardly

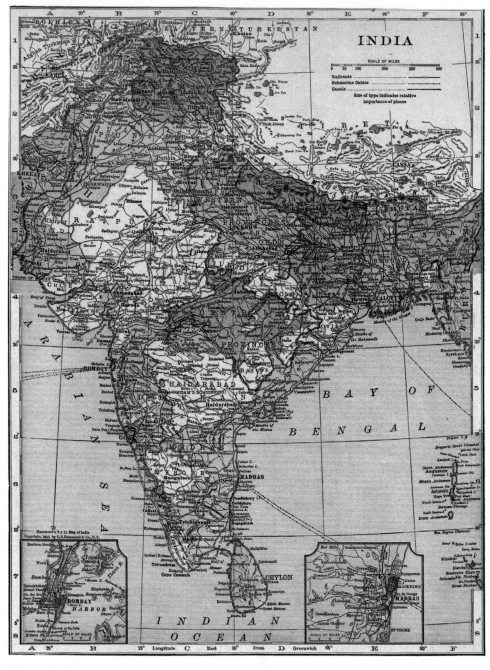

Map of India, circa 1895.

Author's collection

anything to note about my studies, I could only have been a mediocre student."

Mohandas enjoyed storytelling, and one legend had a big impact on his life. He went to see a play about legendary King Harishchandra, and he was riveted watching the actors on stage. The story depicted Harishchandra, a king of ancient India, who was known for telling the truth and keeping his promises. But to test his truthfulness, Harishchandra endured difficult challenges that cost him his kingdom, home, and separated him from his wife and son. When he took up grisly work in a cremation ground, he thought all was lost. But because King Harishchandra was steadfast in his honesty, he was reunited with his wife and son and regained all he had lost. Mohandas was impressed by the message of this play: the importance of telling the truth and keeping one's promises.

MARRIED AT THIRTEEN

Over the following years Mohandas focused on school and family and adjusted to his new life in Rajkot. But everything changed when he was in his first year at Rajkot High School. Mohandas and Kastur were now young teenagers and it was time for them to be married in a traditional Hindu wedding ceremony. The wedding would be held in Porbandar, where Kastur's family and many of Mohandas's relatives still lived.

There was a lot to do in preparation for the big event, which quickly became more complex when Kaba decided to have an elaborate triple wedding.

The British Raj

The term *raj* means "to rule" and comes from **Hindi**, an official language of India. The British Raj means "British Rule," which prevailed throughout the Indian subcontinent from 1858 until 1947, when Gandhi helped India gain its independence from Britain.

The early roots of the British Raj began in 1600 with the formation of the British East India Company (EIC) chartered by Queen Elizabeth I. The EIC was headquartered in London and privately owned by wealthy merchants and aristocrats. The company was formed to trade with the East Indies, but mainly traded with India for cotton, silk, salt, tea, indigo dye, and opium. The EIC competed with the Dutch and Portuguese, who were also interested in lucrative trade with India. The company exercised unfair military rule throughout India until the Indian Rebellion of 1857 (also known as the Great Rebellion, or the First War of Indian Independence), when Indians rebelled and the EIC was abolished.

The following year, with the Government of India Act 1858, the British government began to rule India under Queen Victoria, who was proclaimed the Empress of India. During the raj, various Indian provinces and territories were directly under British authority, while hundreds of separate native Indian states, called "princely states," were governed by Indians but subject to British authority. Kaba Gandhi was a diwan of the princely states of Porbandar and Rajkot. Cultural changes came about gradually in India from the British Raj's impact on India's railway system, legal system, architecture, agriculture, schools, fashion, food, and sports.

Queen Victoria, known as the Empress of India, reigned in England (1837 to 1901) during the same period as the British Raj.
Wikimedia Commons US-PD-Art, 1860

In addition to the marriage of Mohandas and Kastur, the wedding would also include Mohandas's 16-year-old brother Karsandas, his 17-year-old cousin Motilal, and their brides. The wedding would be held in a large banquet hall in Porbandar that would be beautifully decorated with flowers, ornaments, garland, and decorations. Music would fill the air! The whole process of wedding preparations would take months. Invitations needed to be written and hand delivered, and elaborate menus for the wedding feast needed to be drawn up. At 13, Mohandas hadn't thought much about getting

Write a Legend

The Harishchandra legend was one of Mohandas's favorite stories, and it is a popular legend in India today. Legends are tales that help readers learn important life lessons. They're often rooted in a culture's core beliefs and passed down from generation to generation. Legends combine elements of fact, folklore, and fantasy, and they center around a main character, such as King Harishchandra, who encounters difficult trials to overcome. A few American legends include the story of apple farmer Johnny Appleseed, the giant lumberjack Paul Bunyan, and the pioneer Calamity Jane. Try your hand at writing your own original legend.

YOU'LL NEED

* Pen or pencil
* Writing paper

1. Write a legend that is approximately one to three pages.

2. Brainstorm ideas for your main storyline by thinking about a person who encounters big problems. What problems could occur? What is this person up against? Jot down your ideas and choose your favorite theme to write about.

3. Choose a main character (male or female), and give the person a name. Next, describe characteristics about this person such as age, place where he or she lives, what he or she does, appearance, and personality traits.

4. Define your setting and where your story takes place in terms of country, city, or state. You might want to choose your own community as a setting.

5. Come up with a second character (male or female) who opposes your main character and causes all sorts of problems.

6. Now write your story with a beginning (sets up your main character), middle (presents problems for your main character), and end (reveals how your main character is able to confront and solve problems).

7. When you conclude your legend, think about the life lessons your reader will take away from your story.

8. Give your legend a title. Think about sharing your story with friends, family members, or teachers.

married to a girl he hardly knew. He viewed the marriage as a kind of permanent friendship in keeping with Hindu tradition and wrote, "I do not think it meant to me anything more than the prospect of good clothes to wear, drum beating, marriage processions, rich dinners and a strange girl to play with."

When Mohandas and Karsandas arrived in Porbandar for the wedding, they began pre-wedding Hindu rituals. Both brothers smeared a yellow paste of turmeric over their faces and bodies to give a golden glow to the skin. This paste was also thought to enrich the skin and bring good luck and spiritual protection. Kastur was also busy getting ready. She also applied a turmeric, almond, and cream mixture to her skin. She then took a ceremonial bath that was sweetened with herbs and perfumes. Her hands and feet were adorned with intricate designs made with a special ink from henna leaves. On her wedding day, her hair was carefully styled with flowers and jewels, and she wore a beautiful red sari. Kastur's mother placed a red dot called a *bindi* in the middle of her forehead as a blessing, and a gauzy veil was placed over the young girl's head.

While excitement was building for the big wedding, trouble was brewing miles away. Kaba's boss had asked him to stay behind in Rajkot for work, and everyone worried that Kaba might miss the carefully planned wedding day. As the day neared, Kaba left work and raced for Porbandar in the fastest vehicle he could find—a horse-drawn buggy. "Faster, faster!" he kept admonishing the driver to speed on. A wheel of the carriage hit a rock in the road, causing the entire buggy to topple over. Kaba and the driver were shaken and wounded, but alive. When Mohandas's father finally arrived for the wedding, he wore his finest clothes, plus a few newly placed bandages.

A 1915 portrait of Mohandas and Kasturba.
Courtesy of Gandhi Heritage Portal

Create a Henna Hand Design

When Mohandas and Kastur married, Kastur decorated her hands with intricate henna designs. Henna body art, also called mendhi, is an ancient Indian art form also popular in Africa and the Middle East. Designs are made with henna paste, a natural greenish-brown dye made from dried and crushed henna leaves. Henna is believed to bring good fortune and will naturally fade in a few weeks after application to the skin. Create a vibrant henna design using the outline of your hand.

YOU'LL NEED

* Computer with Internet access
* Printer paper
* Pencil with eraser
* Dark brown or black colored pencil

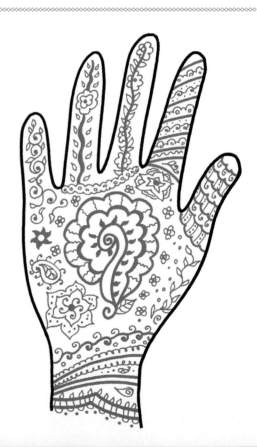

1. Go online and view images of henna designs to brainstorm ideas. One helpful website is Kid World Citizen: http://kidworldcitizen.org/2012/06/07/henna-hands-a-simple-craft/.

2. On paper, trace the outline of your hand with a pencil.

3. With your pencil, draw henna patterns inside the hand outline on each finger, the center of the hand, and the wrist. Common henna patterns use dots, circles, and lines to create flowers, vines, leaves, and paisley.

4. Once your design is complete, retrace and darken the lines with a dark brown or black colored pencil for a finished look.

At last the wedding procession began. The brides were brought to the hall by their parents in three festively arrayed carriages. The grooms rode three decorated horses in a music-filled procession down the streets of Porbandar to the hall. Putlibai and her relatives walked in the parade happily singing wedding songs. Inside the hall, three canopies adorned with flowers had been set up for the three individual marriage ceremonies. Under the canopies, the brides and grooms sat near one another on small wooden stools, along with their parents, as a Hindu priest recited their marriage vows. The last part of the ceremony was called the Seven Steps. Together, Mohandas and Kastur took the first seven steps of their marriage and recited memorized vows. As was customary, the three letters "bai" were added as a suffix to Kastur's first name to indicate she was now a married woman.

Although Gandhi later criticized child marriages, in his autobiography he wrote, "Everything on that day seemed to me right and proper and pleasing." But the wedding night was far from easy. Gandhi said he and his young wife were "two innocent children" who felt shy and nervous and barely spoke. And although they were both coached individually by relatives about basic sex education before their marriage, Gandhi wrote that sexual desires and physical intimacy would come later. Nonetheless, their life as a young married couple had begun, and it would last for more than 60 years.

After the wedding festivities, the large Gandhi family traveled back to Rajkot in ox-drawn carts.

It was customary at the time for Hindu men and women to ride in separate carts, which gave Kasturbai a chance to get to know Putlibai, and her new sisters-in-law. As she headed to a new life that likely felt exciting, Kasturbai brought along a cedar chest filled with new clothes and a teakwood jewelry box of gold bracelets, bangles, rings, and earrings. But it couldn't have been easy for 13-year-old Kasturbai to say good-bye to her parents. As the cart rolled toward Rajkot, Mohandas and Kasturbai probably mulled over many questions—*What will marriage be like? How will we get along? What will our lives be like now?*

TUMULTUOUS TEEN YEARS

Over the next five years, Mohandas continued to attend Rajkot High School while his young wife lived with his family in Rajkot. It was a whole new world for Kasturbai, who had never been outside her hometown of Porbandar. Although she was busy, she felt homesick. She worked and cooked in her new home, went to temple, and visited with friends and family. Kasturbai and Putlibai got along well and enjoyed one another's company. As was customary for the time, the young bride also moved back home to be with her family in Porbandar for many months at a time. Marriage for the young couple meant a great deal of time apart and a chance to mature.

Their relationship developed over time, but not without its trials. Although Mohandas and Kasturbai were attracted to one another and a devoted relationship was blossoming, Mohandas was unsure of how to relate to her. To Kasturbai's surprise and dismay, he became a disagreeable, jealous, and unreasonable husband, saying she could not leave the house without his permission. Strong-willed Kasturbai wanted to please her husband and have a harmonious relationship, but she wasn't about to be homebound and alone. Bitter arguments erupted until Mohandas realized Kasturbai was being a thoughtful and faithful wife, with her own rights and needs. He learned a lesson about respecting her and withdrew his demands.

Mohandas then came up with a new and quite unconventional idea for his wife. He decided he would educate her to help them become closer. Like many girls and women of her time, Kasturbai did not know how to read or write. But the idea of learning these skills made her feel very uncomfortable. Learning to read and write would set her apart from the other women in her family who had not gone to school. Although Kasturbai initially went along with the plan, the lessons were held at night when she was exhausted from long days of work. She wasn't enthusiastic about the lessons and didn't progress in her studies. After a few tutorial sessions, Mohandas let go of this plan.

Mohandas was also changing as a teenager, and he wanted to be independent. He tested the waters with friends and family, took risks, stepped outside his strict Hindu traditions, and sometimes made mistakes. At times he behaved in ways he knew his parents and wife would not like and did things behind their backs. Smoking was first. After seeing an uncle smoke, he thought, *Why not give it a try?* He started smoking his uncle's smoldering cigarette butts and then stole coins from the pockets of household servants to buy new cigarettes. Realizing he didn't like smoking after all, Mohandas gave it up for good. But he still needed to learn a lesson about taking things from others. When he found out Laxmidas was in debt, Mohandas clipped a bit of gold from his brother's armband to pay off the debt. But the pilfering made Mohandas feel awful. Consumed with guilt, he wrote a letter to his father and confessed what he'd done. Kaba respected his son's honesty and quickly and kindly forgave him. Mohandas made up his mind to never steal again.

There were more challenges on the way for Mohandas. In high school he decided to become a meat eater, which went against his strict Vaishnava Hindu vegetarian diet. A persuasive school friend convinced him to eat meat, saying it would make him physically stronger and more assertive. The idea appealed to Mohandas, who wanted to be more robust. He started to eat meat on various occasions throughout the following year. But like smoking, Mohandas realized eating meat wasn't for him. In time, he decided to return to being a vegetarian, and he never ate meat again.

At 16, Mohandas and Kasturbai faced great loss and sadness. Mohandas's father's health continued to decline after the terrible carriage spill three years earlier. As a devoted son, he would race home after school every day to attend to his father, who had become bedridden. Mohandas would change his bandages, give him medicine, massage his legs, and bring him nourishing food or water. One night Mohandas's uncle arrived to give him a needed break. Mohandas left his father's bedside and went to sleep with Kasturbai, who was pregnant with their first child. During this short absence Kaba died, and Mohandas grieved that he had not been with his father when he passed away.

A few days later, Kasturbai's first child was born prematurely, and in his autobiography Gandhi wrote that the "poor mite" lived for only a few days. Filled with grief, Kasturbai returned to her parents' home in Porbandar to rest and heal. After spending time with family and friends, she returned to Rajkot to be with her husband.

After Kaba died, family money started to dwindle. Mohandas's mother and his two brothers, Laxmidas and Karsandas, turned to him for financial support. They all viewed Mohandas as smart, responsible, and capable, and the son most suited to follow in his father's successful footsteps. But this meant he needed to find a solid career that would bring in adequate money for living expenses for his large extended family. He would need to go to college.

In 1887 Mohandas graduated from Rajkot High School and then traveled to the town of Ahmedabad to take his mandatory matriculation exams for acceptance to college. He passed the exams and was accepted to Samaldas College located about 100 miles southeast of Rajkot in Bhavnagar, a coastal city on the Gulf of Khambhat.

During this time, India was becoming a more industrialized country with a new railway system being constructed throughout the subcontinent.

Change was especially evident with old and new forms of transportation existing side by side. To get to Samaldas, Mohandas traveled by both camel and train to arrive in time to start classes in January 1888. At the age of 18, it was the first time he'd ever lived alone, and he missed Kasturbai, who was pregnant again. Although he studied hard at school, he said, "I went, but found myself entirely at sea. Everything was difficult." He was homesick for his wife and family, and left college after only one semester to head back home. But leaving college worried his family because they were counting on him for their future stability.

ONWARD TO ENGLAND

After Mohandas returned from Samaldas, his family gathered to figure out what he should do next. They consulted Mavji Dave, a trusted family adviser. Mavji suggested that Gandhi go to London, England, to study to become a lawyer at the Inner Temple, one of the Inns of Court. Gandhi was excited about the idea, but he explained what he really wanted to do was become a doctor. However, like Gandhi's father, Mavji thought it would be best for Gandhi to become a lawyer. This way, his chances of finding a suitable job in British-ruled India would be much stronger. He could become a diwan just like his father.

But school in England? The family was taken aback with Mavji's suggestion because the idea was so unconventional and potentially improper for their Hindu faith. Although Mohandas's older brothers could see the plan had merit, Putlibai had

Design a Vegetarian Menu for a Day

Although Gandhi experimented with eating meat when he was a teen, he became a strict vegetarian during his college days in London, even avoiding milk and eggs. Later in life, Gandhi started drinking goat milk for his health. Vegetarianism refers to a style of eating in which some or all food products from animals are avoided. Types of vegetarian diets include:

Lacto-ovo vegetarians *eat fruit, vegetables, grains, beans, nuts, seeds, dairy foods, and eggs—but not meat.*
Lacto-vegetarians *eat fruit, vegetables, grains, beans, nuts, seeds, and dairy foods—but not meat or eggs.*
Ovo-vegetarians *eat fruit, vegetables, grains, beans, nuts, seeds, and eggs—but not dairy foods or meat.*
Semi-vegetarians *eat fruit, vegetables, grains, beans, nuts, seeds, dairy foods, eggs, fish, and poultry—but not beef or pork.*
Vegans *eat fruit, vegetables, grains, beans, nuts, and seeds—but do not eat animal products, including meat, eggs, or any dairy products.*
     Some vegans are "fruitarians," eating only fruits, nuts, and seeds.

YOU'LL NEED

❋ Computer with Internet and printer access and printer paper

or

❋ Card stock and pen or pencil

❋ Ingredients and equipment to prepare the food on your menu

1. Use one of the five major vegetarian diets presented above to create a one-day vegetarian menu for breakfast, morning snack, lunch, afternoon snack, and dinner. Think about including brightly colored fruits and vegetables that are red, orange, purple, green, and yellow. These colorful foods provide a number of beneficial nutrients.

2. On the Internet, research various vegetarian websites to find food items and recipes you might use for your menu. You could start with:

BBC Good Food
http://www.bbcgoodfood.com/recipes /collection/vegetarian-kids.
This site has easy-to-follow vegetarian recipes with photographs and instructions.

Meatless Monday
http://www.meatlessmonday.com/favorite -recipes/.
Created by the global Meatless Monday campaign, which encourages people to avoid eating meat on Mondays, this website offers many vegetarian recipes.

3. Go to a library and check out vegetarian cookbooks such as *Vegetarian Kids' Cookbook* by Roz Denny and *Kids Can Cook Vegetarian Recipes* by Dorothy R. Bates.

4. Once you've planned your vegetarian menu for a day, type it up on your computer so it fits on one page and print it out, or write it by hand on printer paper or card stock.

5. Share and prepare your menu with family and friends. How does it compare to your regular meals? What did you like or dislike about it?

My Vegetarian Menu for a Day

BREAKFAST

_____   _____

_____   _____

SNACK

_____   _____

_____   _____

LUNCH

_____   _____

_____   _____

SNACK

_____   _____

_____   _____

DINNER

_____   _____

_____   _____

doubts. How would her son fare in such a strange and distant land rife with temptations that might conflict with their religion?

Mohandas couldn't wait to go. He just needed to figure out how to pay for it. With the help of Laxmidas and Karsandas, he pooled enough money to pay for school in England, and Kasturbai even sold her jewelry to help cover costs. And to reassure his mother, Mohandas took three sacred vows and solemnly promised not to eat meat, drink wine, or consort with women in England. During all this activity, Kasturbai went into labor and delivered a healthy baby boy named Harilal. Happiness prevailed and the entire Gandhi family rejoiced. Everything seemed to be falling into place.

Mohandas would sail from Bombay (now known as Mumbai) to England aboard the SS *Clyde* for about three weeks. The steamship would travel west on the Arabian Sea, through the Gulf of Aden, north on the Red Sea, through the Suez Canal to the Mediterranean Sea, through the Strait of Gibraltar, and out to the Atlantic Ocean, heading north to sail through the English Channel. It would finally dock at the Port of Southampton in England, and from Southampton, he would head to London.

When it was time to leave, Mohandas Gandhi said good-bye to his mother, Kasturbai, baby Harilal, and his many family members. It was a tearful farewell. He then traveled with Laxmidas from Rajkot to Bombay to board his steamer. In Bombay his travel plans started to unravel. Elders of Gandhi's Modh Bania caste discovered he had plans to sail to England. They were vehemently against it, saying he should not go because it would compromise his Hindu religion and caste.

Gandhi wasn't about to give up his plans, and he did not back down. In a surprising move, the elders then excommunicated him from his caste. This action also affected family members, including Kasturbai, who were also cast out by their association with Gandhi. Laxmidas reassured his young brother to continue on his journey to England, and on September 4, 1888, Gandhi set sail for many new and exciting experiences in a foreign country. He would not see his family for three years.

FULL STEAM AHEAD

In Port Porbandar, Gandhi had witnessed many boats and ships of all sizes coming and going. Sailing on the modern SS *Clyde* was his first time on a steamship. Gandhi preferred to be by himself on the crowded ship. Most everyone on the ship spoke English, making it challenging for Gandhi to chat with others. When a steward rang a dinner bell the first evening, Gandhi declined to eat in the ship's dining hall with its fancy tables, chairs, white tablecloths, odd-looking knives and forks, and meat-filled dishes. Gandhi was accustomed to sitting on the floor with family members for meals and using his fingers to eat foods from a round brass platter filled with his favorite vegetarian dishes. He spent a great deal of time by himself in his cabin, eating the sweets and fruits he had brought along.

Even daily hygiene was a challenge. Gandhi would wake early and use the water closet (toilet) before taking a saltwater bath. Passengers were advised not to use soap while bathing because it was nonsoluble in saltwater and made the skin susceptible to ringworm. But Gandhi used soap, feeling it was more civilized to do so, and eventually developed ringworm, which was later cured in London.

Although Gandhi could be painfully shy, he made friends easily and people seemed to gravitate toward him. His cabinmate was an older Indian gentleman named Sjt. (Mr.) Tryambakrai Mazmudar, who was also heading to London to study law. The two got along, and Mr. Mazmudar encouraged Gandhi to be bold, speak up, and work on using the English language, which would help him as a future lawyer.

In time, Gandhi enjoyed being on the steamer, which provided a way for him to transition from the world he knew in India to the world he would discover in England. Along the way, the ship would sometimes dock at different ports, giving Gandhi and other passengers a chance to go ashore and sightsee. Gandhi enjoyed playing the piano for passengers, and in the evenings he would venture up to the deck for fresh air and to marvel at the night sky. "One dark night when the sky was clear, the stars were reflected in the water. The scene around us was very beautiful at that time. I could not at first imagine what that was. They appeared like so many diamonds," he later wrote in his 1888 London diary.

THE LONDON YEARS

Wearing his most distinguished-looking white flannel suit, Gandhi disembarked the SS *Clyde* with Mr. Mazmudar and eagerly went ashore. Culture shock struck immediately. He was soon in the modern metropolis of London, with its large buildings, crowded streets bustling with people, horse-drawn carriages, and bobbies, as the English police are called. When Gandhi looked around at his new surroundings, he quickly saw that

London's bustling Piccadilly Circus, 1890–1900.
Library of Congress
LC-DIG-ppmsc-08577

Englishmen wore black suits—not bright white ones. It was an uncomfortable realization and the first of many learning experiences Gandhi would have as he acclimated to the English lifestyle while studying to become a lawyer at the Inner Temple.

The first night in London, Gandhi stayed in the posh Victoria Hotel. Later that evening, Gandhi met up with close family friend Dr. Pranjivan (P. J.) Mehta, who had come to welcome him to London and to give him helpful advice about lodging. Over the next three years, Gandhi lived in many different places in London. He lived with a roommate, boarded with a family, and eventually found various one-room flats where he could cook his own food.

Wanting to fit in as a proper English gentleman, Gandhi nearly went overboard adopting the dress and customs of the English. He bought a pricey English suit and top hat. He also took violin, ballroom dancing, French, and elocution lessons. And, trying to look dashing, Gandhi admits in his autobiography that he spent too much time in front of a mirror, tying his necktie and combing and parting his hair. After spending his limited funds on these ventures, Gandhi realized it was OK to be himself. He gave up trying to be a Brit. Throughout his efforts to fit in, he didn't give up on his vow to not eat meat, which was no easy task. It seemed that wherever Gandhi went, he was constantly encouraged to eat meat by well-meaning friends. But he stuck to his word and survived many weeks solely on porridge and hot cocoa for breakfast and boiled spinach with bread and jam for lunch and dinner.

Gandhi also started to read local newspapers such as the *Daily News* and the *Daily Telegraph* to learn about London. It would have been hard for him to miss two big stories that dominated the 1888 news. An unidentified killer named Jack the Ripper was terrorizing East London, and young girls forced to work 14-hour days making matchboxes were on strike for better pay and working conditions. The following year Gandhi read about the victorious 1889 London dockworkers' strike,

Gandhi wears English attire as a student in London.
Wikimedia Commons

when thousands of workers marched through the streets of London demanding increased pay and better working conditions. It was a whole different world from Rajkot and certainly eye-opening for Gandhi.

THE CENTRAL VEGETARIAN RESTAURANT

When Gandhi wasn't in class, he enjoyed walking the streets of London in search of vegetarian restaurants. He eventually stumbled upon the Central, a vegetarian restaurant near Farringdon Street, where he devoured his first hearty meal since arriving in town. In addition to providing meat-free food, the Central became an inspiring meeting place for Gandhi. The restaurant sold books, and Gandhi promptly purchased and read *A Plea for Vegetarianism* by Henry Stevens Salt. He later said, "From the date of reading this book, I may claim to have become a vegetarian by choice."

From his connections at the Central, he then became a member of the London Vegetarian Society, where he met and conversed with like-minded vegetarians and prominent intellectuals from the London area. He was introduced to author Helena Blavatsky, who wrote about theosophy—a spiritual philosophy focusing on the divine nature of God, truth, and love. He became acquainted with social activist Annie Besant, who had written about the match girls' strike of 1888 and was also a theosophist like Blavatsky. He also met and worked briefly with famous English author Sir

The Bhagavad-Gita

The *Bhagavad-Gita*, often referred to as the *Gita*, is a sacred and ancient Hindu text composed of 700 **Sanskrit** verses. The book is also called the *Song of God*. The word *gita* means "song," and *Bhagavad* means "God." Although the *Gita* is not a song set to music, its many verses create melodious sounds when spoken. The *Gita* presents a heartfelt conversation between Lord Krishna and Prince Arjuna as they discuss the nature of God and humanity. The book is part of the *Mahabharata*, an epic Sanskrit poem of ancient India.

The *Bhagavad-Gita* has been translated to English by different authors. It was first translated to English in 1785 by Sir Charles Wilkins, a British typographer and scholar of Asia. In 1885, British poet and journalist Sir Edwin Arnold translated the *Gita* as *The Song Celestial*. Gandhi first read Arnold's translation of the *Bhagavad-Gita* when he was in England. The book made a great impact on Gandhi's commitment to nonviolence. Today, the *Gita* is a classic read around the world.

Edwin Arnold, whose book *The Song Celestial*, an English translation of the **Bhagavad-Gita**, made an enormous impact on Gandhi's life.

Gandhi's three years in London were a time of great personal growth, and important seeds were planted for his future work as a lawyer, reformer, activist, and writer. He had a thirst for knowledge, and even though he was shy, he interacted with a wide range of people who had different

Build a Book Exchange Bookshelf

Gandhi loved to read, and many books gave him insights about life and widened his worldview. While in London, friends shared books with him that he would reread throughout his life. In this activity you'll use cardboard boxes to construct a sturdy bookshelf so you can swap and share books with friends, family members, or classmates. Keep the shelf in your bedroom, a family room, or your classroom.

YOU'LL NEED

* 2 corrugated cardboard boxes, 16 by 10 by 8 inches (40.6 by 25.4 by 20.3 cm)
* Scissors
* Masking tape, 2 inches (5.1 cm)
* Recycled newspapers (to protect the floor)
* Craft glue
* 1 sheet of corrugated cardboard, 20 by 24 inches (50.8 by 60.9 cm)
* Pencil
* Ruler or tape measure
* Acrylic paint (white plus a variety of colors)
* Paintbrush
* Computer and printer
* Printer paper
* Index cards

1. Find two sturdy cardboard boxes that are about 16 inches long, 10 inches tall, and 8 inches deep. Recycle used boxes or buy boxes at an office supply store.

2. With scissors, remove the top flaps from both boxes.

3. Use masking tape to close and secure the bottom flaps of both boxes. Tape over all open edges for a clean smooth look.

4. Lay down newspapers on the floor. Place one box on its side (on the newspapers) and pour glue over the top of the box. Let the glue set for 30 seconds.

5. Next, stack the other box on top of the first box to glue the two boxes together. Hold the boxes in place for a few minutes so the glue will start to harden. Place a book on the middle shelf as a weight to hold the boxes together and let them dry for at least two hours or overnight.

6. Once the glue has dried, tape the boxes together along the front, sides, and back to strengthen the entire structure.

7. Next, build the triangular shelf top with the sheet of corrugated cardboard. Measure and cut the cardboard sheet into three equal pieces that are 20 by 8 inches (50.8 by 20.3 cm) in size. On the floor, line up the three cardboard pieces. Leave a ¼-inch (.6-cm) gap between each piece and tape the three pieces together. Trim the excess tape and fold the boards into a triangular form. Tape the entire structure together, and tape all the open edges of the cardboard.

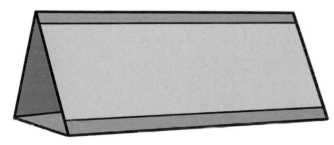

8. Glue the top of your shelf to the stacked boxes (using the gluing method in steps 4 and 5) and let the structure dry for at least two hours or overnight.

9. Next, tape around the triangular top to reinforce the seams. Then tape the top to the shelf so it is firmly attached.

10. Now paint the entire shelf with a white base coat, then apply acrylic paints and let the paint dry. You might like to paint decorative designs on your shelf.

11. Open a document on your computer's word processing program and type BOOK EXCHANGE in a large font and print. You may wish to enlarge these words on a photocopier. Glue the sign to your shelf top. You can also add decorative images from recycled magazines.

12. After stocking your bookshelf with a few books, organize your books by author, title, or subject. In addition, you could create basic guidelines for using your Book Exchange. On index cards, friends and family members can write down the titles of books they've checked out or added to your collection.

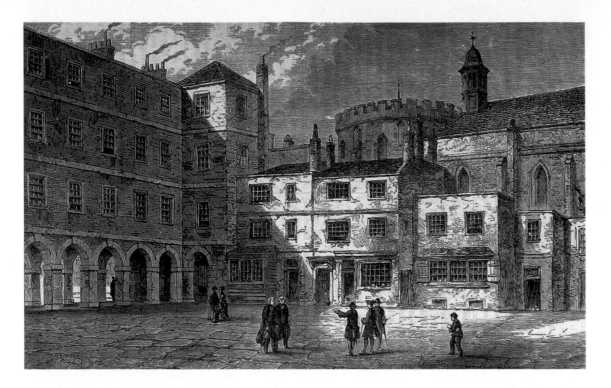

A part of the Inner Temple where Gandhi studied to become a lawyer.

The British Library © The British Library Board, 010349.l.1.

coming together and refusing to accept unjust treatment. And he became a voracious reader. Through sharing books with friends, Gandhi read books including *The Song Celestial* and the Bible. Gandhi was also curious about the works of Russian author Leo Tolstoy, as well as other famous writers.

Gandhi soon developed a burning desire to write. The year he graduated he wrote six articles about vegetarianism that were published in the London Vegetarian Society journal, *The Vegetarian*.

On June 10, 1891, after passing his Inner Temple exams, Gandhi was called to the bar, which meant he was now qualified to argue a legal case in a courtroom. The following day he enrolled in the High Court of London and officially became a lawyer. One day later he set sail for India. He couldn't wait to see his mother to let her know he'd kept his three vows. He was also eager to see Kasturbai and his son, Harilal. In only three years, Gandhi had changed so much. But what would his family think of him now? Most important—would he be able to find work?

worldviews. These experiences opened his mind to new ideas in the areas of vegetarianism, religion, and social reform. He saw how laborers such as the match girls and the dockworkers could go on strike and successfully fight for their rights by

3

A LAWYER AND A REBEL

The only tired I was, was tired of giving in. —Rosa Parks

When Gandhi sailed from England and arrived in Bombay in the summer of 1891, he was nearly 22 years old. He'd been married to Kasturbai for almost nine years. He was the father of a three-year-old son, and he was now a lawyer. Feelings of responsibility must have weighed heavily on his shoulders.

Conscientious Laxmidas, who had become the head of the household and a father figure for Gandhi after Kaba died, was standing on the dock when Gandhi's steamer pulled in. He missed his younger brother and looked forward to seeing him again. But when Laxmidas saw Gandhi dressed like a distinguished English gentleman, he wasn't sure what to think. He wondered if his brother would be able to adjust to the Indian culture after living in England for so long.

The joy of their reunion quickly turned to pain. Laxmidas had the difficult task of informing Gandhi that their mother had died during his final year of law school. Gandhi was heartbroken to hear the news and wrote in his autobiography, "My grief was even greater than over my father's death."

But their lives needed to move forward. At Laxmidas's request, the first order of business was to have Gandhi readmitted to the family's Modh Bania caste. Laxmidas didn't want his younger brother's dismissal from their caste to get in the way of his future career or family relations. Gandhi knew this was still a problem, saying, "The storm in my caste over my foreign voyage was still brewing."

To change this, certain steps needed to be taken. First, Laxmidas took his brother on a pilgrimage to the holy city of Nashik, India, where Gandhi dipped into the sacred waters of the Godavari River as a spiritual cleansing. Next, a ceremonial caste dinner was prepared for Gandhi in a Rajkot banquet hall, and elders of their caste were invited. To make amends, Gandhi served foods to the caste elders. Their acceptance of his food signified his acceptance back into the caste. Once Gandhi's ban was lifted, his family members could all be together again. Although Gandhi appreciated the caste members' continued support, he felt uncomfortable with these rituals, saying, "I did not like all this." But he realized his willingness to comply with his brother's wishes meant more harmony for his family.

Gandhi sits with his brother Laxmidas (on left).
Courtesy of Gandhi Heritage Portal

HOME AGAIN

Wanting Gandhi to feel at ease, Laxmidas made changes in the household to create a more English atmosphere. Suddenly there was fine china and a table and chairs for dining. English foods such as porridge and cocoa were added to the menu.

Mohandas and Kasturbai were happy to be together again, and Gandhi enjoyed playing outdoors and exercising with Harilal and his nieces and nephews. But it wasn't long before he became restless with home life. His insecurities surfaced, and he began to act jealous of Kasturbai as he had when they were first married. After having spent three years in England engrossed in schoolwork, he was once again bent on teaching Kasturbai how to read and write, which upset her. She wanted him to concentrate on his job hunt, pay off his school debts, and bring in money for the household instead of focusing on her education. Conversations got heated, and Mohandas decided it was best if Kasturbai went to visit her parents in Porbandar. He hoped the time apart would help them both cool down.

In a month she returned to Rajkot, and her relationship with her husband improved. The two talked more, and Mohandas admitted he was concerned about his ability to get a job. He worried that his classes at the Inner Temple hadn't prepared him to be an Indian lawyer. He knew a lot about English law, but little about Indian law. Friends suggested that Gandhi head to Bombay, where he could study Indian law, spend time observing court proceedings, and have more job opportunities.

Although it meant leaving his family again, Gandhi left for Bombay and soon found a small apartment to live in. After hunting for work, he was finally hired to handle a case in small claims court. But when Gandhi stood up to cross-examine a witness in the courtroom, his shyness overwhelmed him. He was unable to speak and couldn't even ask one question. Gandhi left the courtroom, and he told his client that he was sorry but he couldn't continue with the case.

Discouraged with the field of law, Gandhi then applied to teach English at a local high school, but he didn't get the job. After six months in Bombay, Gandhi headed back home to Rajkot and set up a small law practice there. He finally started making money by drafting legal documents.

In 1892, a second son named Manilal was born, bringing more joy to the family. Mohandas and

The railway station in Bombay.
© *The British Library Board, Photo 181/(2)*

Kasturbai were finally settling down. And then, as life would have it, things changed all over again.

SAILING TO SOUTH AFRICA

Out of the blue, Gandhi received a letter from Dada Abdulla and Company, a prosperous Muslim shipping and trading firm in Porbandar that had business in South Africa. The firm was involved in a long legal dispute and hoped Gandhi could go to South Africa on their behalf and help settle the matter. The pay would be good, but Gandhi had serious concerns. *Should he leave his family again? How long would the case last? What would the work entail?*

Tempted by the chance to make much-needed money and to visit another country, Gandhi agreed to go. Although he and Kasturbai would miss one another, they were used to being apart. Kasturbai was happy about the prospect of her husband's new job, which was supposed to last only one year. She could handle that.

In April 1893, Kasturbai, Harilal, and Manilal went to the Rajkot train station to say good-bye to Gandhi. It was a sad but encouraging farewell,

Map of South Africa, 1886.

Author's collection

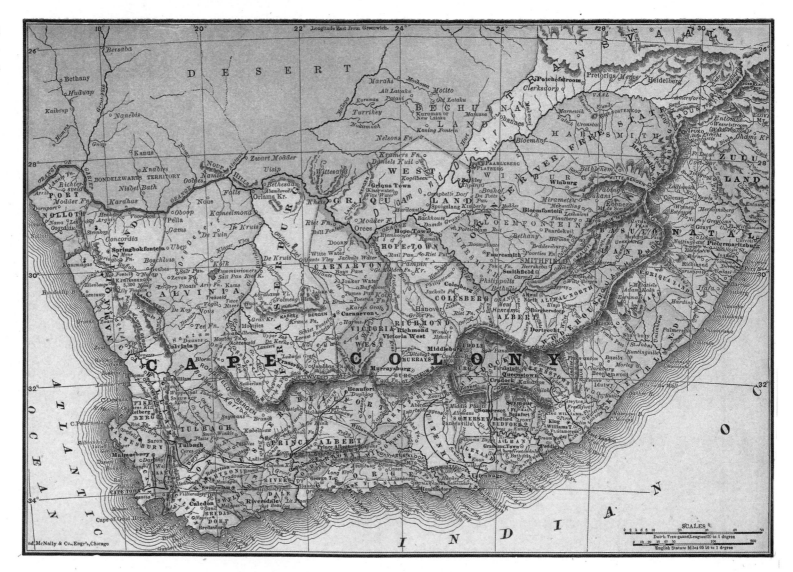

and Kasturbai hoped he was headed in a promising direction. Now 23 years old, Gandhi took the train to the Bombay harbor, where he caught a steamer that sailed west across the Indian Ocean to Port Lamu in Kenya, Africa. From Lamu, the ship sailed south along Africa's eastern coastline to the city of Durban, which was an English colony in Natal, South Africa. The entire trip took one month, and Gandhi arrived during a dry and sunny time of the year.

As his boat sailed into the Port of Durban, also called the Port of Natal, he saw a verdant tree-covered bluff surrounded by blue waters and white sandy beaches. The bluff framed the narrow, picturesque entryway into the harbor. After his boat docked, Gandhi was greeted by Dada Abdulla, the Muslim owner of Dada Abdulla and Company. He was then taken to the company's offices in Durban to learn about the complex legal case that he was hired to work on. In a few days, Gandhi would meet with the company's lawyer in the city of Pretoria, which was located hundreds of miles north of Durban.

When not discussing business matters, Dada Abdulla enjoyed talking about his Islamic faith. In his autobiography, Gandhi wrote, "We had long discussions on religious topics." Dada Abdulla then took Gandhi to visit the Durban court and meet other people involved with his case. Wanting to look professional, Gandhi was dressed in a distinguished European business suit and turban, which he was accustomed to wearing. But when the judge saw Gandhi's turban, he viewed it as

South Africa

With a population of more than 54 million people today, the Republic of South Africa is a unique country with 11 official languages. It is often called the Rainbow Nation for its diversity. Located at the southernmost tip of Africa, its coastline stretches some 1,700 miles, bordering the Indian Ocean on the east and the Atlantic Ocean on the west.

The country has three capital cities: Pretoria (administrative), Cape Town (legislative), and Bloemfontein (judicial). Its government is a representative democracy.

Some of South Africa's early inhabitants were the San, Khoikhoi, Xhosa, and Zulu peoples. In the mid-1600s, the Dutch, known as the Boers, began to settle in the southwest region of the country. Other European settlers followed, including British colonists, who arrived in the early 1800s.

When Gandhi traveled to South Africa in 1893, he settled in the eastern Natal region, which was under British rule. He was quickly subjected to discrimination by whites. Gandhi later lived and worked in the northern Transvaal region, founded by the Boers. His efforts to fight for Indian rights in South Africa were focused in the Natal and Transvaal regions. He remained in the country for nearly 21 years.

From 1948 until 1991, South Africa was divided by **apartheid**, an unjust government system of white minority rule that separated people based on race and skin color. Measures to dismantle apartheid began in the late 1980s. In 1994 Nelson Mandela became the country's first black president, establishing democracy for South Africa.

disrespectful attire for the courtroom and told him to take it off.

Insulted at being asked to remove a personal item that represented pride for his Indian culture, Gandhi left the courtroom with his turban still on. He was again faced with culture shock and realized that South Africa was different from anywhere he had ever lived. In India he felt loved and accepted, and in London he had many English and Indian friends. But what would it be like to live in South Africa?

Dada Abdulla gave Gandhi advice on what to expect and how to interact with others. Gandhi learned there were thousands of Indians living in South Africa, and especially in Durban. Some were "passenger" Indians, like Gandhi, who had paid for their own passage from India to South Africa. Many were indentured Indians, who had been transported to South Africa for work. Some were free Indians, who had completed their work as indentured laborers.

It didn't take long for Gandhi to feel the disapproval of the white ruling class. He had already been offended when asked to remove his turban in court. Not satisfied to let the matter go, Gandhi wrote an article for the local paper, the *Natal Advertiser*, and defended his right to wear a turban.

Various newspaper articles, however, described Gandhi as an "unwelcome visitor" to their town. But like writer Annie Besant, who wrote about the injustices of the young girls making matches in London, Gandhi wrote about his own rights as an individual. In only a few short days, Gandhi had made a name for himself in South Africa. This newspaper article was one of his first steps toward his future work as a writer, activist, and social reformer. But there were rocky roads ahead.

Indentured Indian Laborers

In the mid-1800s, the sugarcane industry in Natal, South Africa, was growing. European plantation owners looked to India to employ low-cost, strong laborers who could work in the hot sun in the fields and harvest the sweet, chewable plant. Between 1860 and 1911, thousands of Indians were brought to Natal as indentured Indians. The term *indenture* refers to a contractual agreement for work. The indentured Indians were given free transport to South Africa, minimal wages, and free food and housing, and were contracted for five years of labor. After five years, the laborers were considered free to remain in the country and own a small plot of land, or to return to India. Some indentured Indians also found employment as domestic workers, or worked in dockyards, railways, or coal mines.

However, living in South Africa as an indentured Indian was difficult. Homes were typically tin barracks, and meals often consisted of rice, lentils, cornmeal, pumpkin, potatoes, and fish. The days were long, the workload was harsh, and pay was minimal. Many indentured Indians were treated abusively and whipped by their employers. Over time, the Natal Government created restrictions, such as insisting indentured Indians pay a high three-pound tax, which made it difficult for them to remain in South Africa even if they wanted to.

REJECTED AND EJECTED

After one week in Durban, Gandhi set out for Pretoria to assist Dada Abdulla's lawyer with the case. To get there, he would travel by train and stagecoach. Having purchased a first-class railway ticket, Gandhi took his seat in a first-class section of the train. About 9:00 that evening, the train stopped at a station in the town of Pietermaritzburg, located about 50 miles north of Durban. A white man on the train saw darker-skinned Gandhi sitting in first class and did not like it. The man returned with train officials, who told Gandhi he had to get up and move to a lower-class train seat. Baffled and angered, Gandhi explained he paid for a first-class ticket, and he refused to move. A policeman then arrived, grabbed Ghandi out of his seat, and threw him off the train.

It was wintertime, and Pietermaritzburg was bitterly cold. Shivering in the station's dark, cold waiting room that night, Gandhi wondered how he would ever get to Pretoria. He even considered quitting the job and moving back to India. But he didn't give up. That night was a pivotal wake-up call in Gandhi's life. He realized the "deep disease of colour prejudice" had to change.

The following day, Gandhi boarded a different train and resumed his journey to Pretoria. But the grief wasn't over. Once Gandhi got to a town named Charlesworth, he boarded a stagecoach to Johannesburg. On the stagecoach, a white conductor told Gandhi he had to sit outside the coach on the footboard. When Gandhi resisted, the conduc-

The Pietermaritzburg train station.
Courtesy of Gandhi Heritage Portal

tor started to shove Gandhi around, box his ears, and yank his arms until other passengers shouted for him to stop. The man finally let Gandhi go. Gandhi wondered if he would reach his destination alive.

After a final train ride from Johannesburg, Gandhi reached Pretoria. The following day he met Dada Abdulla's lawyer, Mr. A. W. Baker, an English attorney and devout Christian working on the case. The two men got right to work. Gandhi pored over legal documents and helped translate the clients' native Gujarati language to English.

Investigate Authors Who Inspired Gandhi

Gandhi was very open to new ways of thinking and doing things in his ongoing efforts to live simply, strive for nonviolence, and work for Indian rights. He often turned to books to learn about others' ideas. Like his father, he was open to meeting people and discussing new approaches and ideas. For this activity, investigate key authors who influenced and inspired Gandhi from his teenage years and beyond.

YOU'LL NEED

* ❋ Computer with Internet access
* ❋ Library access
* ❋ Paper
* ❋ Pencil or pen

1. Visit your local or school library, or go online to research some or all of the following individuals and their books:

   Sir Edwin Arnold, author of *The Song Celestial*

   Annie Besant, author of *Why I Became a Theosophist*

   Helena Blavatsky, author of *The Key to Theosophy*

   John Ruskin, author of *Unto This Last*

   Henry David Thoreau, author of the essay "Civil Disobedience" and the book *Walden*

   Leo Tolstoy, author of *The Kingdom of God Is Within You*

2. What do you think Gandhi learned from these authors? How are these authors' ideas alike or different? What books and authors have influenced *your* life?

3. Jot down ideas or quotes that inspire you.

During breaks from work, Gandhi had many conversations with Mr. Baker about religion. Gandhi was very curious about different faiths, and he had a deep desire to learn about a wide variety of religions such as Christianity, **Buddhism**, Islam, Jainism, Judaism, and Theosophy. He read books, talked with others, attended religious gatherings, and thought about what did or did not resonate with him and his Hindu faith.

Gandhi also thought about basic human relations and how unkindly he'd been treated since arriving in South Africa. Other Indians told Gandhi they were also treated disrespectfully in South Africa—they were not allowed to walk after dark without a special pass, they were not allowed to stay or eat in certain hotels or dining rooms, and they were rarely allowed to travel in anything but the lowest-class sections on public transportation.

BECOMING A LEADER

Gandhi saw the need to help Indians living in South Africa, who were too often treated with disdain and disrespect. He contacted Indians in Pretoria and invited them to a meeting in town. Gandhi later wrote, "My speech at this meeting may be said to have been the first public speech in my life." Standing before the group, his nervousness disappeared and his words flowed freely.

Gandhi gave his audience members advice about living in South Africa. He talked about being truthful in business matters, improving their cleanliness and hygiene, and making it a priority to learn the English language. The group was grateful for the gathering and agreed to meet once a month to talk about problems and solutions.

Gandhi then wrote a letter to the South African railway authorities to let them know how cruelly Indians were treated on trains. This letter made a difference. Gandhi received news saying first-class tickets would be issued to Indians who were properly dressed. Gandhi shared the news at a following meeting.

In 1894, after one year, the Dada Abdulla and Company lawsuit was finally over. Gandhi had been invaluable in helping the two opposing sides reach an acceptable, fair settlement. During this important year in Gandhi's life, he had learned a great deal about being a lawyer and having success. Now it was time to return home to India to be with his family again.

From Pretoria, he returned to Durban, where friends gave him a daylong going-away party. During the festivities, Gandhi picked up the local *Natal Mercury* newspaper and read an article titled "Indian Franchise" about a proposed government bill to restrict voting rights for Indians in Natal. Gandhi was shocked, knowing this was wrong. He immediately alerted others. Suddenly the farewell party turned into a work session with heated discussions. Guests implored Gandhi to please stay in South Africa to help fight for their voting rights. Gandhi agreed to stay on for a month, and he immediately wrote a petition to fight the bill.

Thousands of Indians signed Gandhi's petition, which described the mistreatment of Indians, and copies of the document were sent to newspapers in South Africa, India, and England.

Although leading newspapers supported the Indians' demands, the bill passed anyway. Now Gandhi truly had his work cut out for him. He wrote to Kasturbai to let her know that he needed to remain in South Africa to help. Gandhi, who was now about 25 years old, set up a small law office in Durban and got to work.

THE NATAL INDIAN CONGRESS

In May 1894, Gandhi founded the Natal Indian Congress, a community organization set up to fight for Indians' rights. It was Gandhi's first step into the world of politics. He wanted Indians to have a voice in social and political matters. Word soon spread throughout the Natal Indian community of the young lawyer named Gandhi who cared about them.

One day an indentured Indian named Balasundaram showed up at Gandhi's door desperately seeking help. He wore tattered clothes, was timidly holding his turban, and his mouth was bleeding because his two front teeth had been knocked out. Balasundaram told Gandhi he had been severely beaten by his employer. Gandhi kindly told the man it was OK to put his turban back on. After listening to his story, Gandhi then sent him to a doctor. Gandhi informed a local judge about the incident, and he eventually helped Balasundaram find a new job. In time, Gandhi helped convict the abusive employer.

Soon, Gandhi was making a very positive difference for Indians who needed legal help. Over the next 20 years he fought for the rights of indentured laborers and against the unjust taxation of Indians who decided to stay in the country. Gandhi learned how some Indians who had been recruited to work in South Africa had eventually bought homes and land and developed flourishing businesses. But some white businessmen didn't like this competition and were angry about it. The three-pound tax against the indentured Indians was designed to make it difficult for them to stay and prosper in South Africa.

SIX MONTHS IN INDIA

In 1896 Gandhi returned to India for six months to let key people know about the harsh conditions for Indians in South Africa. He also set out to prepare his family to move to South Africa. It was a busy time of travel, meeting others, writing, giving presentations, and attending to community and family matters in Rajkot.

During the short stay, Gandhi wrote a controversial publication called the *Green Pamphlet*, which outlined the disrespect shown to Indians in South Africa. The pamphlet was distributed to newspapers in India, England, and South Africa, and eventually got him into deep trouble when some South Africans didn't like what the pamphlet said. But now in India, other problems seemed to mount. The deadly bubonic plague had broken out in Bombay, and as a preventive measure, Gandhi worked to improve sanitation facilities in Rajkot to stop the potential spread of the plague in his family's hometown. Sadly, his sister

Create an Anti-Bully Poster

When Balasundaram sought out Gandhi, he was frightened and needed serious help. Balasundaram had been attacked and harassed by his boss over and over again. Fortunately Gandhi stepped in and helped this bullied man confront his abuser. For a great deal of his life, Gandhi worked hard to stop abuse by empowering suppressed and mistreated people to stand up for their rights. Bullying is common in our society today, whether it's done outwardly or anonymously, in person or via cyberspace. To help prevent and bring awareness to the problem of bullying in your community, create an anti-bully poster that will pack a peaceful punch and send a powerful message.

YOU'LL NEED

* Computer with Internet access
* Printer paper
* Pencil
* Poster board, 22 by 28 inches (56 by 71 cm)
* Images
* Craft glue or glue stick
* Colored markers

1. Think about when and where bullying may have occurred in your life. Brainstorm ideas to help prevent bullying. You can check out anti-bullying websites such as PACER Center's Kids Against Bullying at www.pacerkidsagainstbullying.org/kab, or Stopbullying.gov-Kids at www.stopbullying.gov/kids/.

2. Come up with a theme for your poster by addressing an issue that matters to you. Think about where you hope to see bullying stop.

3. Now create a slogan for your poster that says a lot in just a few words.

4. Sketch out how you'd like your poster to look, with words and images. Draw your own images or add some from a recycled magazine. Use markers to add color.

5. Share your poster with your family, teachers, or people in your community.

Raliatbehn's husband became very ill at this time and died.

STORMY DAYS AHEAD

In December 1896, Gandhi set sail for Durban, South Africa, once again. This time he brought along Kasturbai, Harilal (8), Manilal (4), and Raliatbehn's son Gokaldas (10). The family sailed aboard the *Courland* steamer, which was traveling alongside the *Naderi* steamer. Both steamships were owned by the Dada Abdulla and Company.

About four days from Durban, monsoon winds and powerful waves threatened to capsize the ships. Passengers were frightened for their lives, and Gandhi worked hard to comfort and reassure them. The storm eventually passed, but when the two ships set anchor in the Port of Durban, passengers faced more difficulty. They were told the boats were quarantined to make sure no one would bring bubonic plague, the epidemic in Bombay, into the country. No one would be allowed off the ships until local officials permitted it.

Day after day the passengers waited onboard in the harbor. However, Gandhi discovered there was another reason passengers could not disembark. Some white officials in Durban had learned about Gandhi's controversial *Green Pamphlet* and were angry. They feared Gandhi was stirring up trouble in South Africa and had brought along hundreds of Indians to protest racial discrimination in the country. Gandhi told the officials he was not planning a protest; he was simply bringing his family to Natal.

The passengers were finally allowed to disembark. But when Gandhi got off the ship, a mob of whites, soon joined by six angry white men, shouted, "Gandhi! Gandhi!" and proceeded to brutally kick him and pelt him with rotten eggs, stones, and brickbats. Thankfully, the wife of the Natal police superintendent intervened and courageously stood between Gandhi and the attackers, who then ran off.

Later that night a crowd of angry whites stood outside the home where Gandhi was staying and continued to terrorize him. Donning a disguise, Gandhi managed to escape and seek refuge at the police superintendent's home. Although Gandhi's attackers were about to be arrested, he chose to not press charges, which helped restore peace.

BEACH GROVE VILLA

Gandhi moved his family to Beach Grove Villa, a posh European-style two-story, five-bedroom home with a large veranda that overlooked the Durban bay. The Gandhi family lived here for the next four years, and their family continued to grow and change. A third son, named Ramdas, was born in 1897, and a fourth son, Devdas, was born in 1900. Gandhi assisted in the birth of Ramdas. And then, after reading a book about how to deliver a baby, Gandhi helped his wife deliver Devdas. Kasturbai's role as wife, mother, and respected matriarch of the household was also changing. She would now be called Kasturba.

Gandhi spent long days building his law practice in Durban and working for Indian rights. In time he became a highly respected, well-paid lawyer. He also worked hard to create a home life he felt was best for his family. Gandhi wasn't happy with the segregated or religious-based schools in Durban and chose to homeschool Harilal and Gokaldas during their years at Beach Grove Villa. But this didn't please Kasturba, and the boys wanted to go to school.

In another effort to change their homelife, Gandhi also dismissed all the servants at the villa and expected family members and guests to pitch in and help. He set strict rules for household chores. One new rule upset Kasturba. Gandhi wanted everyone to carry their own chamber pot and dispose of their own waste outside the house every morning. A chamber pot was a portable toilet kept under the bed. Kasturba felt demeaned having to do this lowly task, which had customarily been done by untouchables in India. A huge fight erupted. Gandhi grabbed Kasturba's arm, yanked her out of the house, and threatened to throw her out the gate of Beach Grove Villa. Kasturba pleaded with him to calm down, and he eventually did.

In reflection, Gandhi realized he needed to have more control over his temper. He vowed to change and to be more considerate of other people's feelings and needs. They agreed to be more civil to one another, and over time, Kasturba accepted the chamber pot rule.

THE BOER WAR

In October 1899, a conflict called the Second Boer War broke out in South Africa. The British and the Dutch fought over valuable gold and diamonds that were being mined in the Transvaal region. The Second Boer War lasted nearly three years, from 1899 to 1902, and the Boers eventually surrendered to the British.

A family portrait, circa 1897. From left: Gokaldas, Manilal, Kasturba, Ramdas, and Harilal.
Courtesy of Gandhi Heritage Portal

Make Rangoli Sand Art

Rangoli art is an ancient Indian folk art in which mandala-like designs are carefully created on floors, courtyards, or entranceways using colored sand or rice. A rangoli design is considered a symbol of good luck. This intricate type of sand art has fleeting beauty and is meant to last only a short while to illustrate the beauty and transience of life. Now you can create your own rangoli with colorful sand.

YOU'LL NEED

* Poster board, 22 by 28 inches (56 by 71 cm)
* Two circular objects (such as plates), about 10 inches and 7 inches (25 cm, 18 cm) in diameter
* Pencil
* Ruler
* Three cups, 3¾ inches, 3¼ inches, 2½ inches (9.5 cm, 8.3 cm, 6.4 cm)
* Colored sand (three different colors, 28-ounce bags from craft stores)
* Three small containers to hold sand. Note: small bowls or plastic containers work well.
* Teaspoon
* Fork
* Camera (optional)
* Closeable plastic bags

1. Place your large 10-inch plate facedown on poster board and trace around it with a pencil.

2. Remove the plate and use a ruler to measure and draw a horizontal and a vertical line through the circle to quarter it.

3. Center the smaller 7-inch plate facedown in the middle of your circle and trace around it. Remove the plate.

4. Next, center the 3¼-inch cup facedown in the middle of your second circle—trace around it and remove.

5. Pour each color of sand into a separate bowl or plastic container.

6. Following the largest circle, slowly spoon out about one teaspoon of sand at a time from your container until a ring of sand encircles your circle.

7. Now it's time to move the sand with your cups. First, place your largest 3¾-inch cup at the north point of your circle inside the ring of sand. Slowly push the sand up and outward about 3 inches (7.6 cm) to form a curve like the petal of a flower. Continue using your cup this way at the east, south, and west points of your circle. After you have created four petals, continue moving your sand ring outward with your cup to form more petals.

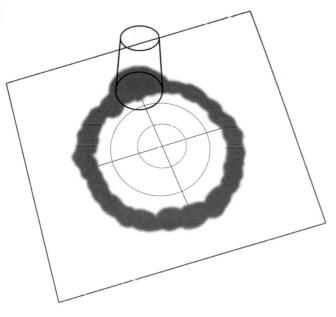

9. Finally, add a new sand color to your smallest circle and repeat, moving the sand about 2 inches (5.1 cm) with your 2½-inch cup. You can sprinkle more sand in the center to add more color.

10. After your rangoli is formed, add texture by dragging a small fork across the sand from the center flower to the outer petals.

11. At the center of your rangoli, use your fork to make small decorative swirls.

12. Sand art is delicate and can be disrupted, so a good way to preserve it is with a photo.

13. To recycle your sand, carefully roll your poster board and empty the sand into a closeable plastic bag. Empty remaining containers of sand into separate closeable plastic bags.

8. Next, add a new color of sand to your second circle and repeat, moving the sand about 2 inches (5.1 cm) with your 3¼-inch cup.

Although Gandhi empathized with the plight of the Boers, who had a much smaller army than the British, he decided it was best to align with the British army. Gandhi wanted to help the British, but he didn't want to fight or use a weapon. He decided to create the Natal Indian Ambulance Corps to work alongside the British Red Cross. Gandhi recruited hundreds of Indians living in South Africa to help.

For nearly six weeks, Gandhi and his team helped carry wounded or killed British soldiers on stretchers from the battlefields, particularly during the Battle of Spion Kop in Natal. Gandhi's first-aid efforts were appreciated, and he and other Indians were awarded British war medals for their service. But, according to Arun Gandhi, in his book *Kasturba: A Life*, "Mohandas had seen enough senseless carnage to confirm forever his hatred of war and violence."

In 1901, while the Second Boer War was still raging in South Africa, Gandhi and his family moved back to Rajkot, India. Although Gandhi reassured his colleagues in South Africa he would return if ever needed, India was their home once again. The Gandhi family had been away for about four years, and their homecoming brought opportunities to be with family and friends again. Harilal and Gokaldas would be able to go to school, and everyone would have a chance to enjoy familiar Indian traditions and customs they'd grown up with.

Once back home, Gandhi and Kasturba were praised for their overseas travel as well as Gandhi's work in law and in the ambulance corps. So much had happened for the couple, who had now been married nearly 18 years. They were very glad to be back in India. But how long would their time in India last?

Gandhi's ambulance team during the Second Boer War. Gandhi is third from right, second row.
Wikimedia Commons

4

THE ASHRAM LIFE

No scene is continually and untiringly loved, but one rich by joyful human labour; smooth in field; fair in garden; full in orchard; trim, sweet, and frequent in homestead; ringing with voices of vivid existence. —John Ruskin

Whether it was where he lived, what he ate, the clothes he wore, the work he did, or even his approach to his health and family life, Gandhi led a unique life. There were many influences in Gandhi's life, including his friends, family, colleagues, books, religion, community, and what was happening in the world around him. Gandhi often experimented with new ways of doing things, and it was quite common for him to move from country to country and place to place.

SOUTH AFRICA REVISITED

One year after the Gandhi family returned to India in 1901, Gandhi received word from the Natal Indian Congress that prominent British statesman Joseph Chamberlain was about to visit South Africa for the first time. Chamberlain wanted to help smooth relations between the British and the Boers after the Boer War ended. But Indians worried how Chamberlain's visit would impact them. They asked Gandhi to return to Natal and meet with the statesman on behalf of Indian rights.

Once again, Gandhi left his family behind as he traveled back to South Africa to help. This time he brought along his nephews Chhaganlal (21) and Maganlal (19), who hoped to find jobs in South Africa.

Gandhi fully expected to return to India within the year, but his plans soon veered in a different direction. His meeting with Chamberlain was disappointing because the statesman had little to say about correcting Indian discrimination. This setback didn't thwart Gandhi's efforts. His next step was to open a new law practice in the large city of Johannesburg, located about 300 miles northwest of Durban. His clients would be among the 12,000 Indians who lived there.

The year 1903 brought big changes for Gandhi and his family. Kasturba and their three youngest sons traveled back to South Africa to be with Gandhi, while Harilal and Gokaldas remained in India to go to school. The family moved into a large home outside Johannesburg.

That same year, a new business venture caught Gandhi's eye. On a visit to Durban, he met with an Indian printer who talked about the idea of publishing a newspaper specifically for South African Indians. It would be a helpful way for Indians

(*left*) British statesman Joseph Chamberlain.
Library of Congress LC-DIG-ggbain-03487

(*center*) Gandhi (center) worked for many years as a lawyer in South Africa.
Wikimedia Commons

(*right*) Gandhi as a lawyer in 1906.
Courtesy of Gandhi Heritage Portal

to read the news, learn about issues related to their lives and work, and voice their opinions about important topics. Gandhi loved the idea and began writing the paper, which he named the *Indian Opinion*.

The newspaper was published in both Gujarati and English. After a long day of legal work, Gandhi would switch gears and write articles for the *Indian Opinion* before sending them off to Durban. He now juggled two jobs: as a lawyer in Johannesburg and a newspaper writer for the *Indian Opinion* in Durban.

WORKING TOWARD SIMPLICITY

When Gandhi was working as a lawyer in South Africa he made more money than he had ever known. His family's upscale homes at Beach Grove Villa and in Johannesburg reflected this. But deep down, Gandhi questioned the value of his upper-class lifestyle and wondered how he could simplify his life.

Over time, his ideas about money and materialism changed—sometimes out of sheer necessity. When a white barber in Pretoria wouldn't cut Gandhi's hair because he was dark skinned, Gandhi figured out how to cut his own hair. Instead of sending out his clothes to be laundered at high prices, Gandhi learned how to wash and iron his many shirts and collars by himself. He figured out how to do things on his own, and he also taught Kasturba and their sons how to be self-sufficient.

What Is an Ashram?

An ashram is a unique homestead, settlement, or retreat that offers its residents a place to live, work, play, go to school, and worship in a chosen setting. Ashrams have similarities to monasteries or communal settlements and are typically established in rural or mountainous settings far from the hustle and bustle of urban life.

Ashrams have a long history in India and are often based in Hinduism. Today, there are ashrams all over the world that provide residents a place to focus on spiritual beliefs and explore activities such as **yoga**, meditation, music, dance, and art.

Yoga is often practiced at ashrams.
Shutterstock, Pikoso.Kz

Little by little, Gandhi was moving toward a more independent and simplified existence that would eventually lead to a new way of life—living in ashrams.

Practice Anti-Consumerism for a Day

Can you reduce your possessions for a day? Can you take a pause from all your products? Many of us live in a world overflowing with stuff that goes way beyond our basic needs. Material possessions—clothing, accessories, beauty products, jewelry, electronics, games, toys, books, and bikes—can take up a lot of room in our lives.

YOU'LL NEED

* Paper
* Pen or pencil

For this activity, spend a day using and consuming as few material goods as possible. You don't need to cut back on food intake for this activity, but try to pare down the number of products you use, starting first thing in the morning. Use a journal to keep track of your anti-consumerism day. For example, when you wake up in the morning, what do you do first? Do you turn on a light? Do you put on a robe or hoodie? Do you reach for your mobile phone or computer? Do you get your glasses? Do you brush your teeth? Write it all down, item by item.

Think about activities that do *not* involve material things, such as taking a walk or singing. Make a list. At the end of the day, describe what happened in your journal. How did it feel to be more conscious of the many products you use every day? Were you surprised by all the products you use? What could you do without? How could you simplify your life? What did you do that did not involve a material item? What product-free activities could you do more often in your life?

You might enjoy sharing this journal with a family member, friend, or teacher to see what they have to say. Consider writing an article about your anti-consumerism day for a local newspaper or your school newspaper or website.

THE PHOENIX SETTLEMENT

Gandhi's legal work in Johannesburg was going well. But the *Indian Opinion* newspaper started to have serious financial problems during its early years. Gandhi took a train to Durban to see how he could save the newspaper. To pass time on the long train ride he read *Unto This Last*, a controversial book by English author John Ruskin that challenged society's basic values. This book changed Gandhi's life.

Published seven years before Gandhi was born, *Unto This Last* talked about the value of every individual in a community, fair wages for all, the importance of simplifying one's life, and working with one's hands. *Unto This Last* was an immediate catalyst in Gandhi's life. In his autobiography he wrote, "I determined to change my life in accordance with the ideals of the book." The book inspired him to start his first ashram according to some of Ruskin's innovative ideas.

It occurred to Gandhi that to save the failing *Indian Opinion*, he could move the newspaper office and printing press to a rural setting where people could live and work on the paper in one location. In a matter of days Gandhi purchased 100 acres of beautiful farmland in the town of Inanda, about 15 miles northwest of Durban and two miles from the Phoenix train station.

Surrounded by sugarcane fields, the land seemed ideal. It had a spring to provide water, fields for growing food, and an orchard with orange, mango, and guava trees. With the help of friends and relatives, Gandhi constructed a large

building for the *Indian Opinion* newspaper. And there was enough land for families to build simple homes of wood and corrugated metal on spacious lots. Residents would farm their own fields and

John Ruskin

Born in 1819 in London, England, John Ruskin was a Victorian writer, artist, art critic, and philosopher. He was considered a prominent sage and social reformer of his time. In addition to his artwork, Ruskin wrote essays, books, and poetry about a wide range of subjects that focused on art, nature, architecture, spirituality, and social reform. In 1860 he published a series of controversial essays in the *Cornhill* magazine. In them he criticized social norms and industrialism. The essays were later published as a book, *Unto This Last*, in 1862.

In later life, Ruskin's interests turned toward improving the ills of society. He detested how industrialism turned beautiful cities into dingy, disease-infested places. In the 1870s, Ruskin founded the Guild of St. George, which became a homestead dedicated to sustainable farming, craftsmanship, equality, and his desire to make the world a more just and precious place.

John Ruskin wrote the book *Unto This Last*, which inspired Gandhi.
Library of Congress LC-DIG-ds-04729

Try Out Basic Yoga Poses

Yoga is an ancient exercise method that originated in India thousands of years ago. It works with the body, mind, and spirit to help people relax and reduce stress while building strength. Yoga improves basic muscle tone, flexibility, and balance through a variety of poses and breathing techniques. There are different styles of yoga such as hatha, vinyasa, and bikram.

YOU'LL NEED

- ❋ Comfortable clothes
- ❋ Yoga mat (optional)

1. Try out the following basic yoga poses. It will be most comfortable on a carpeted floor or a yoga mat. Remember not to force a pose that feels uncomfortable. See if you can take a yoga class in your community to learn more.

Easy pose. Sit on the floor and cross your legs pretzel style. Keep your back straight, and align your feet beneath your knees. Now, place your palms on your knees, look straight ahead, and relax your neck and shoulders. Close your eyes if you like. Breathe deeply.

Tree pose. Stand with your feet hip-width apart. Now, shift your weight to your left leg and lift and bend your right knee, turning it out to the right. Rest your right foot against your left ankle or calf. Slowly drag your foot up your left leg to your left thigh, working to maintain your balance. Once you feel stable, slowly bring your palms together at your heart before raising both arms straight up. Breathe deeply. You can try the tree pose on the other side too, balancing on your right leg and drawing your left knee up.

Cobra pose. On the floor, lie on your stomach with your legs stretched out behind you. Now, press your legs and feet into the floor, keeping them close together. Place your hands under your shoulders and lift your head and shoulders away from the floor, keeping your arms slightly bent or straight. Keep your legs straight as you look forward or slightly upward. Typically your back will bend slightly while you are in cobra pose. Take a few deep breaths.

Downward-facing dog pose. Get on your hands and knees on the floor. Straighten your arms without locking your elbows. Now lift your hips and straighten your legs. Press your heels toward the floor and look toward your feet in this upside-down V formation. Take a few deep breaths. From this pose you can move to the child's pose and relax.

Child's pose. Get on your hands and knees on the floor, and then sit back on your feet. Stretch your arms straight out in front of you with your palms on the floor. Your stomach should rest on your thighs with your forehead touching the floor. Take a few deep breaths and relax.

learn typesetting to help with printing the newspaper. All workers would earn equal wages. Chhaganlal and Maganlal moved to the new settlement and helped with running the printing press as well as farming and preparing foods in a community kitchen.

In 1904, Gandhi named the small ashram the Phoenix Settlement. The ashram was an innovative idea that truly appealed to Gandhi and likely reminded him of a communal village of Trappist monks he had once visited near Durban, where the residents lived, worked, and worshipped on site.

Gandhi's family wouldn't move to the Phoenix Settlement until 1906. However, at their home in Johannesburg, they continued to simplify their lives. Family members took turns using an iron hand mill to grind wheat into flour for nutritious homemade bread. Gandhi continued to homeschool his sons and encouraged them to help with chores and tend a small garden outside their home. The boys would often walk miles with their father to and from his law offices, which gave them time to be together and talk. Gandhi often used this time to teach the boys basic school lessons.

Over the next few years, Gandhi continued to live and work in Johannesburg to make money to support his family, the *Indian Opinion*, and the Phoenix Settlement. He was now affectionately called "Bapu," which was a Gujarati term of endearment that honored him as a father and leader.

HELPING THE ZULUS

Gandhi and his family moved frequently throughout their lives from different continents and countries, to different cities, homes, and ashrams. It was probably both exciting and exhausting to constantly adjust to new places. The family often moved with Gandhi to wherever he felt he was needed most, especially during times of conflict.

In 1906, a revolt broke out between the Zulus, a South African people living in Natal, and the British colonists who had ruled the Zulus since the late 1800s. In the early 1900s the British started to tax the Zulus, which the Zulus saw as harsh, unjust, and unwanted. Resentment and anger grew among the Zulus. Violence broke out when

Zulu chief Bhambatha kaMancinza.
Wikimedia Commons

Visit a CSA Farm

Fruits and vegetables were grown on all of Gandhi's ashrams, while goats and cows provided dairy products. Gandhi wanted his ashram communities to be self-sufficient so food was always available. Today, Community Supported Agriculture (CSA) is an alternative way to produce food, and an example of self-sufficiency in farming that focuses on locally grown foods. There are tens of thousands of CSAs around the world. With the CSA farming method, people who live in a community can obtain a wide variety of food by investing in and/or helping work on the CSA farm.

YOU'LL NEED

* ❋ Computer with Internet access
* ❋ Library access
* ❋ Paper
* ❋ Pen or pencil
* ❋ Camera (optional)

1. Go online or visit your local or school library to research the names of CSAs in your community. You can also check out the website Local Harvest: "How to Visit a Farm" at www.localharvest.org/organic-farms/visiting.html.

2. Write down contact information for a CSA you'd like to visit. Contact the farm by phone or e-mail and ask when it would be a good time to stop by for a visit. Ask family members or friends to join you, or organize a school field trip.

3. At the CSA, investigate how the farm is organized and run. Who owns the CSA? How many community members work on the farm for food? How much is an annual subscription to this CSA? How are foods provided to community members? Is the farm associated with a community farmer's market?

4. Take photos to document your visit to a CSA.

Vegetables grown via Community Supported Agriculture in the United States. *Author's collection*

Gandhi's ambulance corps during the Zulu Rebellion. Gandhi is seated in the second row, fourth from right.
Wikimedia Commons

Zulu chief Bhambatha kaMancinza took revenge and attacked a white tax collector. The British retaliated and a bloody battle ensued that became known as the Zulu Rebellion or the Bhambatha Rebellion.

When Gandhi heard about the uprising he offered to form a new volunteer ambulance team to help. This meant moving to the Phoenix Settlement, which was closer to the conflict in Natal. Kasturba agreed to move, but she wasn't sure what she was getting into at this new place. She worried her home would be a "wild, snake-infested outpost in the midst of miles and miles of sugarcane fields."

Kasturba and the boys moved to the settlement—and Gandhi set off with his ambulance corps to help. He had his work cut out for him. Because whites didn't want to touch or help the wounded Zulus, Gandhi and his men stepped up to treat the injured. Gandhi discovered, to his dismay, that the so-called war was more of a "man-hunt," and many of the Zulus had festering wounds from being whipped by some of the whites, versus having battle injuries. Although Gandhi didn't speak the Zulus' Bantu language, he said, "from their gestures and the expression of their eyes they seemed to feel as if God had sent us to their succour [aid]."

It was a discouraging time for Gandhi, who walked many miles from village to village in search of injured Zulus. He saw firsthand how horribly violent humans could be to one another. At times Gandhi walked some 40 miles a day, which gave him a lot of time to think about his life. He thought about his future and wondered how he could best use his time and energy to serve his community. He remembered how difficult childbirth had been for Kasturba and realized he didn't want to father more children.

In his autobiography, Gandhi noted that during these long walks he decided to make big changes in his marriage by taking the vow of **brahmacharya**. This vow meant he would become celibate and no longer have sexual relations for the rest of his life. When he told Kasturba about his decision to take this vow, Gandhi wrote in his autobiography, "She had no objection."

EMERGING IDEALS

When Gandhi returned home to the Phoenix Settlement after six weeks helping the wounded Zulus, his ideas about nonviolence began to crystallize. He wanted to work toward finding more peaceful ways to resolve conflicts, especially for Indians. Many people admired Gandhi's work toward Indian rights and wanted to join in and help. Over the next four years, Gandhi's family lived at the Phoenix Settlement. But he realized a much larger ashram would be needed to provide a safe home for the many individuals who wanted to take part in his peace and justice movement. The new ashram would be named after a famous novelist.

TOLSTOY FARM

In 1910, the Tolstoy Farm was established on 1,100 acres located 22 miles from the city of Johannesburg, and Gandhi's family soon moved there. The farm, nearly 10 times the size of the Phoenix Settlement, was donated by Gandhi's longtime friend Herman Kallenbach. A German-born Jew who was an architect and fellow vegetarian living in South Africa, Kallenbach named the ashram after Russian novelist and philosopher Leo Tolstoy. Gandhi had long admired Tolstoy's book *The Kingdom of God Is Within You*, a Christian-based book about nonviolence.

The large farm had a pristine setting of fertile land and a vital water supply. Nearly 1,000 orange, apricot, plum, peach, fig, almond, walnut, acacia, and eucalyptus trees grew on the property, and water was supplied from a spring and two wells. A railway station was located about one mile from the farm. Three main buildings were constructed to provide shelter for some 70 to 80 adults and children. The ashram became a diverse community of people of different backgrounds, races, and religions. Emphasis was on simple living, self-sufficiency, and community harmony. Residents spoke different languages such as Gujarati, Hindi, and English, and respect for different religions at the farm was encouraged. In time, many people participated in Gandhi's future work in nonviolence.

Days on the Tolstoy Farm revolved around set routines. Residents were expected to pitch in to help sustain the community with the basic necessities of food, clothing, and shelter. The farm also provided residents daily nondenominational prayer services, exercise, and school. Drinking

A main building at the Tolstoy Farm near Johannesburg, South Africa.
Courtesy of Gandhi Heritage Portal

and smoking were prohibited at the ashram, and although vegetarianism was preferred, meat eating was allowed. There was plenty of farm work to do, including planting, tending, and harvesting crops. Residents spent a great deal of time preparing foods that they grew in abundance on the large acreage. They made sweet marmalade from oranges, creamy nut butter from groundnuts, and home-baked breads from flour ground by hand from grain. A tailor shop was set up to sew clothes for the residents, and sandals were made on site.

Chores were never ending. Ashram members washed and put away dishes and swept and cleaned rooms. Gandhi was a stickler for sanitation and insisted that rubbish be buried in trenches, food scraps composted for manure, and wastewater used as water for trees. Residents deposited human waste and covered it with dirt in a square pit dug near the house.

Children were expected to help with chores and to work as a team with others. In his book *Satyagraha in South Africa*, Gandhi explained that children felt good about pitching in with chores, saying, "No more work was given to them than what they willingly and cheerfully rendered, and I never found that the work thus done was unsatisfactory either in quantity or quality."

Children were also schooled on the farm. Gandhi and Herman Kallenbach provided instruction for young people with lessons in sandal making, carpentry, gardening, writing, arithmetic, history, geography, and music. Living on the farm often offered rich learning experiences. For example,

there were many snakes around Tolstoy Farm, and Kallenbach started to read about snakes to learn which ones were poisonous and which ones were beneficial to crops. He once found a venomous cobra and kept it in a cage with the hope of taming it. With patience and a gentle manner, Kallenbach trained the snake to take food from his hand. Gandhi and the children enjoyed watching and learning about the cobra until one day it escaped the cage and slithered away.

Regardless of snakes, many residents at Tolstoy Farm slept outside on porches or in tents. Gandhi believed in the benefits of fresh air and sleeping outdoors:

> It follows that one should make it a point to sleep in the open. Sufficient covering should be used to protect oneself against the inclemencies of the weather—against the cold and dew. In rainy season an umbrella-like roof without walls should be used for keeping the rain out. For the rest, the starlit blue canopy should form the roof, so that whenever one opens one's eyes, he or she can feast them on the everchanging beautiful panorama of the heavens. He will never tire of the scene and it will not dazzle or hurt his eyes. On the contrary, it will have a soothing effect on him.

FITNESS AND HEALTH

Gandhi was a high-energy person, and being fit and healthy mattered to him. As a college student, he had gotten a lot of exercise walking around London, and he continued to walk for exercise for his entire life. In historic photos, Gandhi is often seen walking with others or alone. On his ashrams, Gandhi saw the benefits of hard physical work and exercise through daily chores such as clearing the land, plowing fields, weeding, harvesting crops, picking fruit from trees, and fetching water from the spring or wells.

Although Gandhi had a number of serious illnesses during his life, being healthy was a high priority. Part of Gandhi's health regimen was closely linked to what, when, and how he ate. Although he had a slim physique, in his autobiography he said he enjoyed eating and typically ate a lot of food. As a vegetarian, Gandhi derived vital nutrients for his body through a variety of nonmeat foods such as grains (rice, wheat, oats, corn); legumes (peanuts, pulses, lentils, beans, peas); roots and tubers (potatoes, carrots, yams); and nuts (walnuts, almonds, pistachios), along with many other fruits and vegetables. Although he abstained from milk for a number of years, he did drink goat milk and consume dairy products such as butter, ghee, and curds.

Gandhi was very attuned to how he felt, and he experimented with different kinds of diets throughout his life. At one time he went on a "fruitarian" diet, eating only fruits and nuts. Another time he ate only five foods a day. Like his mother, he sometimes fasted and didn't eat for days or weeks. He believed it was best to not eat overly salty or spicy foods, or too much sugar.

KEY TO HEALTH

Gandhi was a prolific writer and wrote many books. One of his favorite subjects to write about was health. In 1906, when Gandhi was in his late 30s, he wrote articles for the *Indian Opinion* newspaper under the headline "Guide to Health." In 1942, in his early 70s, Gandhi wrote an 83-page booklet called *Key to Health*, published in 1954 in different languages. At the start of *Key to Health*, Gandhi wrote, "The inner working of the human machine is wonderful. The human body is the universe in miniature."

In the book, Gandhi dedicated chapters to the human body, air, water, food, condiments, tea, coffee, cocoa, smoking, alcohol, and drugs. Gandhi also wrote about sexuality, brahmacharya, and natural health cures such as mud poultices, castor oil packs, and hydrotherapy to help with everything from fevers to scorpion bites. Although Gandhi had strong opinions about many subjects, he encouraged individuals to think for themselves and "do as their heads and hearts may dictate."

He enjoyed reading and learning about medicine and often had his own ideas about health and wellness that leaned toward natural cures, which could be unconventional for the time. For example, Gandhi read about the natural health benefits of earth poultices, which were compresses made with specially prepared, sterile mud. When Ramdas broke his arm when he was five, Gandhi wrapped his son's arm with a strip of moistened, mud-covered fabric. After a month of this daily mud-wrap treatment, Ramdas's arm healed. When Gandhi suffered from constipation, as he occasionally did, he sought relief with mud poultices placed on his stomach.

Gandhi also believed in hydrotherapeutic hip or sitz baths to bring down a fever. When Manilal was very ill with pneumonia, Gandhi had him sit for a few minutes in a shallow tub of water at intervals throughout the day. He also wrapped his son in a cool wet sheet mummy style, which exposed only his head. Shortly after this sheet wrap, Manilal's fever broke.

Gandhi had many alternative approaches to life in his efforts to become self-sufficient, raise his children, work toward social justice, and lead a simple, healthy, and meaningful life. His ideals and efforts continued to develop as he turned toward the philosophy for which he would become recognized the world over—nonviolence.

THE POWER OF NONVIOLENCE

Peace is available in every moment, in every breath, in every step. —Thich Nhat Hanh

By the time Gandhi was in his mid-30s, he had already witnessed or experienced a great deal of violence. He had been thrown off a train in Pietermaritzburg and harassed and beaten by a mob of whites at the Port of Durban. He had met and helped indentured Indian Balasundaram, whose boss had beaten him and knocked out his teeth. And he had seen people barbarically wounded, whipped, or killed during the Second Boer War and the Zulu Rebellion.

Gandhi tried to make sense of the violent behavior he saw around him, which gnawed at his soul. Although he was a reserved and introspective person, he wrestled with his own angry feelings, especially with family members.

Like his father, Gandhi could be a strict and demanding person. He remembered when he lost his temper with Kasturba because she didn't want to empty chamber pots. He was sometimes at loggerheads with his first son, Harilal, over school issues. Gandhi hoped there might be a better way for people to get along and stop all the violence.

FINGERPRINT YOUR CHILDREN

After the Boer War ended, the British took control of the Transvaal region, and Gandhi wrote that "all laws adversely affecting the Indians began to be more and more strictly enforced day by day." In 1906, while Gandhi was working in Johannesburg and his family was getting settled at the Phoenix Settlement near Durban, he read about an ordinance in the August edition of the *Transvaal Government Gazette Extraordinary*. The ordinance outlined how Asians were supposed to sign up with the Registrar of Asiatics office in the Transvaal.

Gandhi quickly realized the ordinance would greatly impact Indians, who made up the majority of Asians living in the Transvaal. Specifically, the ordinance outlined how Indian and Chinese men, women, and children (eight years and older) were to provide their name, race, age, height,

fingerprints, residence, and names of family members for identification purposes. If Asians failed to register and get a certificate of registration, they would not be allowed to live in the Transvaal and could be penalized with fines or prison time or be deported to their home countries. Asians would be expected to carry and show these registration cards to police officers in public places, or even in their homes, whenever they were asked.

As Gandhi translated the ordinance from English to Gujarati for publication in the *Indian Opinion* newspaper, he said, "I shuddered as I read the sections of the Ordinance one after another. I saw nothing in it except hatred of Indians." Gandhi felt

(*left*) Gandhi begins to work as a nonviolent protester.
Wikimedia Commons

(*right*) The Empire Theatre in Johannesburg.
Courtesy of Gandhi Heritage Portal

that if this ordinance passed, it would be very difficult for Indians to live, work, and raise families in South Africa.

The next day, Gandhi held a meeting in Johannesburg and told a few prominent Indian leaders about the ordinance. The Indian leaders were shocked to learn about it and realized that mandatory registration in the Transvaal could easily be required for all Indians throughout South Africa. Something needed to be done.

UNITE TO FIGHT

To discuss the registration ordinance, a large public gathering was held in the Johannesburg Empire Theatre. Along with journalists and Transvaal government officials, nearly 3,000 Indians took seats or stood in the aisles to learn more about the mandatory registration. People were angry about being forced to register, and many were outraged and offended that women and children would also be required to register. Speaker after speaker addressed the audience.

When Gandhi got up to speak, a hush fell over the crowd as people listened intently to his words. Gandhi encouraged Indians to oppose the mandatory registration as a unified group and not resort to violence. He hoped Transvaal officials would get the message and quickly abolish the restrictive ordinance. However, he informed the crowd that people who resisted the mandatory registration might be up against hard times and should prepare for the worst.

We might have to go to jail, where we might be insulted. We might have to go hungry and suffer extreme heat or cold. Hard labour might be imposed upon us. We might be flogged by rude warders [guards]. We might be fined heavily and our property might be attached and held up to auction if there are only a few resisters left. Opulent today we might be reduced to abject poverty tomorrow. We might be deported. Suffering from starvation and similar hardships in jail, some of us might fall ill and even die.

The very next day fire destroyed the Empire Theatre, where the Indians had met. Although the circumstances were suspicious, the fire was considered an accident. Nonetheless, thousands of Indians staunchly pledged to refuse to register as required by the Transvaal Asiatic Registration Act, which became known as the Black Act. A number of Indians, along with Gandhi, then met with Transvaal government officials and expressed their dislike of the ordinance. But their efforts were in vain; the Black Act was passed in 1907.

SATYAGRAHA TAKES FORM

Gandhi could see that many Indians wanted to resist registration and fight for their rights and freedoms as a unified force. He had been referring to their efforts as "passive resistance," but he didn't feel the term was quite right. He needed a better term. Gandhi then created a contest in the *Indian Opinion* and invited readers to coin a name

Write a Peace Pledge

Gandhi had a remarkable ability to incite change and empower people to fight for their rights. He gave speeches, wrote articles, came up with campaigns against injustice, fasted, and marched for freedom, and he was even jailed for defending his beliefs through protests. He also asked followers to adhere to pledges of nonviolence. A pledge, like an oath or a vow, is a promise to stick to an ideal you believe in. For this activity, write a first-person pledge that would help you contribute to peace, whether it's with your friends or within your family, neighborhood, school, community, or world.

YOU'LL NEED

* Printer paper
* Pen or pencil
* Scissors

1. First, think about nonpeaceful acts or violent behaviors you see around your community or world and write them down.

2. Now, come up with a list of peaceful acts and nonviolent behaviors you like. Think about ways you could help create a more peaceful, nonviolent world. Use your list to write your pledge. Start with, "I pledge to . . ." and fill in the thought.

3. You could also ask friends or family members to write a pledge of their own.

for his nonviolent resistance movement. Gandhi's nephew Maganlal came up with the clever name *sadagraha*, which combined two Gujarati words to mean "firmness for a good cause."

Gandhi liked the word *sadagraha* and slightly altered it to **satyagraha**, which means "firmness for truth and love." Indians who wanted to peacefully fight for their rights would now be called *Satyagrahis*, and Gandhi's nonviolent movement would be called Satyagraha.

In July 1907, permit offices were opened throughout the Transvaal for Indians to register and be fingerprinted, as they were now legally required to do. But Gandhi, who had set up Satyagraha headquarters at his law office in Johannesburg, directed Satyagrahis to resist registration fearlessly and peacefully. Although a few Indians chose to register, most Indians decided to boycott registration and simply not register. Indians stayed on top of the news about upcoming resistance activities by reading the latest editions of the *Indian Opinion* newspaper.

Two leading Transvaal authorities, Prime Minister Louis Botha and Jan Christiaan Smuts, head of Transvaal Indian Affairs, watched Gandhi's Satyagraha movement closely. Both men were prominent Boer War generals and thought Gandhi's resistance movement would eventually lose steam and fade away.

But when thousands of Indians continued to resist registration month after month, Botha and Smuts enforced a final cutoff deadline to register by November 30, 1907. And when Indians still did not register by the cutoff date, Gandhi and many Satyagrahis were summoned to court and arrested. In January 1908, Gandhi and the Satyagrahis were sentenced to two months in a Johannesburg jail, without hard labor. It was the first of numerous jail sentences for Gandhi throughout his life.

In jail, Gandhi was segregated from white prisoners and given a dirty uniform to wear. He was held with the other Satyagrahis behind a thick cell door as if they'd been locked up in a safe. Gandhi was served corn mush—called mealie pap—in the morning, rice and bread for lunch, and mealie pap and vegetables for dinner. As the days went on, more and more Satyagrahis were arrested and jailed. A jail designed to hold 50 inmates now housed nearly 150 prisoners.

Kasturba was living at the Phoenix Settlement near Durban at the time. Since moving to the settlement in 1906, she was often left alone to care for her family while Gandhi lived and worked in Johannesburg and focused on the Satyagraha movement. Kasturba had no idea that Gandhi had been jailed. She was busy at home giving a party to welcome the arrival of their first grandchild. Harilal had married a young woman named Gulab when he was in India, and the couple had moved to South Africa to live at the Phoenix Settlement. Gulab was now in her seventh month of pregnancy, and it was traditional to celebrate at this time.

But the celebration became somber when Kasturba received a telegram informing her that Gandhi was in jail. Devastated, she shared the alarming news with family and friends at the

(*above*) Jan Christiaan Smuts, center row, fourth from right, during the Second Boer War.
Wikimedia Commons

(*left*) Louis Botha during the Second Boer War.
Wikimedia Commons, Project Gutenberg eText 16462

Gandhi was jailed many times throughout his life.
Shutterstock, Mopic

party. Everyone worried about Gandhi's safety, and they feared he was suffering while in prison. Kasturba lost her appetite. At that moment she decided to share in her husband's hardship from afar. She would eat the same corn mush as Gandhi for every meal until he returned.

DID SOMEONE SAY COMPROMISE?

It wasn't long before police escorted Gandhi from his jail in Johannesburg to Pretoria to meet with General Smuts. The general had a plan he thought might work and wanted to discuss it with Gandhi. Smuts assured Gandhi that the Black Act would likely be abolished if most Indians would volun-

tarily register, versus being forced to register. Wanting to compromise and free the Satyagrahis, Gandhi agreed to Smuts's plan with some fine-tuning of the compromise to make sure the Black Act would be repealed. After being imprisoned for about three weeks, Gandhi was then freed from jail along with the other Satyagrahis.

Now it was time to voluntarily register. Gandhi decided to be one of the first Satyagrahis to register and be fingerprinted. But his decision to do this did not please everyone. When a man named Mir Alam, one of Gandhi's Indian clients, found out that Gandhi had decided to register, he felt angry and betrayed. Alam thought Gandhi had gone back on his word. He came to the conclusion that Gandhi had been bribed by General Smuts for money.

What happened next was tragic. Alam, along with a few other Indians, angrily beat, kicked, and knocked out Gandhi. Although the men were arrested for the assault, Gandhi did not press charges, saying, "Those who have committed the act did not know what they were doing. They thought that I was doing what was wrong."

Many Indians continued to trust Gandhi's guidance and voluntarily registered. They agreed to sign up, be fingerprinted, and get their official registration cards. Unfortunately, General Smuts did not keep his word—the Black Act was *not* abolished. Gandhi was shocked and felt he'd been lied to. He sent many letters to General Smuts imploring him to keep his word and get rid of the Black Act as he promised he would. But General Smuts would not back down.

As a result, there was intense and renewed interest in Gandhi's Satyagraha movement. Harilal traveled to Johannesburg to join the struggle. In an act of protest, Harilal intentionally set out to get arrested by selling fruit in Johannesburg without a seller's license. As expected, Harilal was jailed for a week of hard labor. After he was released, the police ordered him to leave the Transvaal. When he refused to leave he was jailed again for a month of hard labor.

Gandhi was fed up and knew something dramatic needed to be done. He sent word to General Smuts with a fierce ultimatum. If the Transvaal authorities did not abolish the Black Act by August 16, 1908, Gandhi and the Satyagrahis would burn their registration cards. General Smuts chose to ignore Gandhi's words *and* his deadline.

A FIERY STATEMENT

On the designated day in mid August, Gandhi, along with thousands of Indians, showed up at a mosque in central Johannesburg where a large cauldron had been set up to burn nearly 2,000 Indian registration cards. Gandhi addressed the large crowd, saying, "By burning the certificates we only declare our solemn resolution never to submit to the Black Act, and divest ourselves of the power of even showing the certificates."

Even Gandhi's attacker, Mir Alam, was there to burn his card. When Alam stood before the crowd and told them he was wrong to assault Gandhi, everyone cheered and applauded. Gandhi and Mir Alam shook hands as a gesture of goodwill. Next,

the many registration cards were thrown into the cauldron and set ablaze. As the flames leaped into the air, everyone cheered again. It was a triumphant moment for Satyagraha and a dramatic demonstration of nonviolent protest. Journalists who covered the event for English newspapers compared the August 16, 1908, card burning in Johannesburg to the 1773 Boston Tea Party, when American colonists defiantly tossed British tea into the Boston Harbor in an act of protest.

JAIL FOR JUSTICE

The card-burning ceremony got attention, but unfortunately nothing changed. The Black Act was still enforced. And to make matters worse, the British continued to clamp down against Indians with new restrictions and taxes, making it hard for them to live and work in the country. Gandhi decided to ratchet up his efforts, fully aware that it would land him in jail. To protest against the Black Act, Gandhi got himself arrested again in 1908 for not having a registration card. This time he was sent to a prison in the town of Volksrust for two months of hard labor. In 1909, Gandhi was arrested yet again and sent to a jail in Pretoria for three months of hard labor. It was his longest sentence so far and the worst jail conditions Gandhi had ever experienced.

When Manilal was 16, he joined the Satyagraha movement and was arrested and sent to jail like his older brother Harilal. The South African newspapers, including the *Indian Opinion*, were constantly informing readers about the Satyagraha movement and how often Satyagrahis, such as Mohandas, Harilal, and Manilal Gandhi, were sent to jail year after year. It was very difficult for Kasturba to watch her husband and sons go to jail. The cruel and restrictive anti-Indian legislation presented more and more opportunities for Indians to protest peacefully and firmly, and to suffer the consequences. The overarching goal was to fill South African prisons with many Indians to make a strong statement about injustice.

Once Gandhi was released from the Pretoria jail in 1909, he set sail for England to alert British officials to the unjust conditions of Indians in South Africa and enlist help from abroad. When British officials offered little help, Gandhi was angered, and he expressed himself through writing. On his way back to South Africa from England, Gandhi wrote an entire book in the cabin of his steamship. The book was titled **Hind Swaraj**, which means "Indian Home Rule." *Hind Swaraj* outlined Gandhi's beliefs about the problems of British dominance and rule, and it suggested solutions toward Indian self-reliance and self-rule.

In 1912, help for the Indians' struggle in South Africa came from India. Gopal Krishna Gokhale, a high-ranking leader who was part of the Indian

Ahimsa and Nonviolence

When Gandhi created his Satyagraha movement, he integrated key ideals of **ahimsa**, a concept he learned about as a young boy growing up in Porbandar and Rajkot. Ahimsa is an ancient spiritual concept of the Jain, Hindu, and Buddhist religions. The word *ahimsa* is commonly translated to mean "to cause no injury and to do no harm." It applies to all living creatures, and beliefs say that to hurt another is to hurt oneself. Ahimsa means seeing all life as sacred, and having peaceful thoughts, feelings, and actions. It goes beyond not using physical violence and fighting. A person who is demonstrating ahimsa is in a constant and compassionate mindset of love toward everyone and everything.

Gopal Krishna Gokhale.
Wikimedia Commons

Independence Movement, came to South Africa and toured the country to better understand the Indians' situation. Gandhi admired Gokhale as a mentor and friend, and it was the first time an Indian leader had visited South Africa to help. In Johannesburg, Gokhale stayed in Kallenbach's home, as well as at the Tolstoy Farm.

Gokhale met with Boer officials, including General Smuts, to work toward Indian rights. He specifically requested that the highly unfair three-pound tax on indentured Indians be abolished. Unfortunately, Smuts did not abolish the tax. Gandhi summed up his thoughts about the treatment of Indians and said, "On the one hand there were the Boer Generals determined not to yield even an inch of ground, and on the other there was a handful of Satyagrahis pledged to fight unto death or victory. It was like a war between ants and the elephant who could crush thousands of them under each one of his feet."

After his visit to South Africa, Gokhale returned to India. He viewed Gandhi as a leader who could one day return to India to help fight for the country's independence. In the meantime, the Indian struggle in South Africa continued, and the government imposed new and stricter immigration laws. It now became illegal for Indians to cross borders, from the Transvaal into Natal or from Natal into the Transvaal, without permits. On top of it all, in 1913 the Supreme Court of South Africa ruled that non-Christian marriages, specifically Hindu and Muslim marriages, would no longer be legally valid. When Mohandas and Kasturba heard this they were outraged. Kasturba

Write a Poem of Ahimsa

Writing poetry is one way to change the world. For this activity, write a poem about ahimsa, an ancient word that means "nonviolence toward all things." Think about living in a world where there is no violence—an ahimsa world. Can you imagine such a place? How would you describe it?

YOU'LL NEED

* Paper
* Pen or pencil

1. Brainstorm ideas of what you'd like to express in your poem. Awaken your imagination. Visualize. How would you explain the concept of ahimsa to a friend, a sibling, or someone from a different country? What does ahimsa mean to you? Where do you see ahimsa in action in your everyday life?

2. Choose the type of poem you'll write. Will your poem rhyme or be free verse? Will it be long or short? It's up to you!

3. Begin the writing process. Come up with a title and then start to put your thoughts down on paper. After your first draft is complete, read your poem aloud and make revisions you think would improve it.

4. Put your poem aside for a day or so and then look at it again later with fresh eyes. Are there changes you'd like to make?

5. When you're happy with your poem, share it with others if you like.

wanted to pack her bags and go home to India. But instead, they both fought back.

WOMEN JOIN THE FIGHT

Since 1906, hundreds of Indian men, including Gandhi's sons and close friends, had been steadily participating in the valiant Satyagraha movement. After seven years of watching friends and family go to jail, and now infuriated by the restrictive marriage laws, many Indian women joined the fight. Like men, women could also get arrested by intentionally selling fruit or vegetables without licenses or by defiantly crossing borders without permits.

Gandhi had read about women suffragists in England and the United States participating in protest marches to fight for their civil and voting rights. Gandhi knew women could be strong. He set into motion a bold plan that enlisted the help of Indian women from both the Phoenix Settlement and Tolstoy Farm. He called the women from the Phoenix Settlement the "Invaders," and the women from the Tolstoy Farm the "Tolstoy Sisters."

In 1913, four Indian women and 12 Indian men, including 15-year-old Ramdas, set out from the Phoenix Settlement to march north across the Transvaal border from Natal without permits. They were led by Kasturba!

(below) The jail in Pietermaritzburg where Kasturba was imprisoned.
Project Gateway South Africa

(right) Kasturba joins her husband as an activist.
Courtesy of Gandhi Heritage Portal

All 16 Indians, including Ramdas, were arrested and sent to jail in Pietermaritzburg for three months of hard labor. The Invaders were the first women to be arrested as Satyagrahis. It must have been hard for Kasturba to watch Ramdas be taken to jail. Plus, she had her own worries about being behind bars.

About the same time, 11 Tolstoy Sisters marched south across the border from the Transvaal into Natal, but they were *not* arrested. Gandhi had advised the Tolstoy Sisters to continue marching onward to the coal-mining town of Newcastle if they were not arrested. So they did. In Newcastle, the women encouraged indentured Indians who were working in the mines, abused and subjected to the unfair three-pound tax, to go on strike. When local police found out, the Tolstoy Sisters were soon arrested and sent to the same jail in Pietermaritzburg where Kasturba was held for three months of hard labor. News of their arrests spread like wildfire.

GOING ON STRIKE

When the coal miners found out women had been imprisoned, they threw down their tools, headed into town, and went on strike. Gandhi immediately set out for Newcastle to join the strikers. The strikers wasted no time in telling him how brutally they'd been treated. One miner showed Gandhi the thick scars on his back where he'd been mercilessly whipped.

Soon, hundreds of Indians quit their jobs and left their modest dwellings to follow Gandhi and

Many indentured Indians march for justice.
Courtesy of Gandhi Heritage Portal

go on strike. Having no place to live, the laborers, along with their wives and children, carried bundles of belongings on their heads and camped outdoors. Generous Indians from Newcastle provided them with food.

Gandhi came up with a plan. He would lead his able-bodied strikers on a 36-mile march from Newcastle to the town of Charlestown in Natal, which was located on the border of the Transvaal. Once at Charlestown, the strikers would illegally cross the border into the Transvaal and likely be arrested. Gandhi made it clear to the marchers there were serious risks in the protest. He reassured the group that no one was required to strike, and they were free to leave the march and return to work if they so desired.

Gandhi then gave the marchers important instructions. Strikers were to respect others' belongings, the protest was to be nonviolent, and strikers were not to resist arrest. If the strikers were attacked, they were to bear the pain and not fight back. Last, Gandhi said, in the event he was arrested, the strikers were to continue marching on.

The large marching caravan left Newcastle on October 28, 1913, and headed to Charlestown. Surviving on daily rations of bread and sugar, the strikers eventually made it to Charlestown. Here, women and children were lodged in the homes of Indians who lived in the small town, while men camped outside. Understanding the importance of the march, the strikers were calm, respectful, and helpful. Gandhi wrote that feelings of love were aroused during the march, and Christians, Jews, Hindus, and Muslims were all brothers. But the government was angry about the march, and there were rumors of police taking up arms and shooting strikers.

During the march, Gandhi was in communication with Transvaal authorities, hoping to avert any trouble and settle the matter peacefully. He let them know that if the unjust three-pound tax were abolished, the strike would be called off. But General Smuts wanted nothing to do with the leader or his march. So, on November 6, 1913, the marchers started walking toward the border of the Transvaal, and Gandhi wrote, "The pilgrim band was composed of 2,037 men, 127 women and 57 children."

The large group crossed a small stream to bravely enter the Transvaal, and many women courageously carried their children in their arms. Policemen mounted on horses stood menacingly at the border gate, but they did not shoot or arrest anyone. Gandhi calmly instructed the group to walk on to Tolstoy Farm. Over the next few days, Gandhi was arrested twice and freed on bail to rejoin his marchers. The third time he was arrested, he was sent off to jail for nine months.

Without their leader, the strikers continued marching toward Tolstoy Farm. Unfortunately, they were eventually stopped by police, herded onto trains, and sent back to Natal to be jailed. Because having so many protesters in jail overloaded the prison system, the South African government forced many of the men back to the coal mines, where they were made to work under police patrol like slaves. The men who resisted were whipped, beaten, or shot. Eventually news of the strike, arrests, and brutality spread across the globe to leaders in India and England, who were outraged. It was time for change.

General Smuts met with Gandhi once again in Pretoria. The two leaders, at long last, agreed on a settlement that granted South African Indians important rights. The Indian Relief Act of 1914 was passed, which abolished the unjust three-pound tax for indentured Indians and validated the country's Hindu, Muslim, and Parsi marriages. In addition, some of the strict immigration demands of the Black Act were relaxed. With these social reforms, Gandhi was satisfied that Indians had achieved critical civil rights to improve their lives. He had stuck to his commitment of nonviolence and now it was time to go home.

On July 18, 1914, Gandhi and his family left South Africa for good. They boarded the *Kinfauns Castle* steamer in Cape Town for a two-week journey that would take them around western Africa and north to England. Gandhi and Kasturba would first visit London before eventually returning to India. Leaving wasn't easy, and Gandhi wrote, "it was a great wrench for me to leave South Africa, where I had passed twenty one years of my life sharing to the full in the sweets and bitters of human experience, and where I had realized my vocation in life."

But there were great new adventures, harsh struggles, and freedoms yet to be won—in India.

Houses of Parliament in London, England, circa 1890.
Library of Congress LC-DIG-ppmsc-08560

6

SPINNING AND FASTING

Gandhi did not merely say "no" to the imported textile that was destroying our textile industry; he put everyone to work spinning cloth. The spinning wheel became the symbol of Indian independence. —Vandana Shiva

After leaving South Africa for India, Gandhi and Kasturba visited London first. Gandhi wanted to meet with his mentor Gopal Krishna Gokhale, who was in town at the time. Gandhi was no longer practicing law and wanted to talk with Gokhale about what he should do next. Unfortunately, his mentor was away in France for medical reasons.

But Gandhi and Kasturba were still glad to be there. It was the first time Kasturba had been to England, and their visit gave Gandhi a chance to show his wife where he'd gone to college and to dine at some of his favorite vegetarian restaurants. And there was a lot more than sightseeing and reminiscing going on in London. War had come to town.

On August 4, 1914, just a few weeks after Gandhi and Kasturba left South Africa, England officially entered World War I. London was abuzz with patriotic fervor. Scores of men and boys volunteered to fight for their country. Patriotic songs and impassioned war slogans such as "Men of the Empire to Arms!" "Unity Is Strength!" and "For the Peace of the World!" fanned the flames of war.

Many people thought the war would be over soon. But it dragged on for four years, from 1914 to 1918. Battles were fought primarily on European soil and resulted in more than 16 million deaths. At the start of World War I, the Allied powers of England, France, and Russia fought against the Central powers of Austria-Hungary, Germany, and the Ottoman Empire. Over the following years, many other countries, including the United States, joined the global battle.

Wanting to help with the war effort, Gandhi began to recruit volunteers for a third Indian ambulance corps. With his newest corps, Gandhi felt he could participate in World War I in a nonviolent way and show his ongoing loyalty to England. But because Gandhi had spent years promoting concepts of nonviolence in South Africa, some viewed his ambulance corps as part of the war effort and thus contradictory to his basic values of satyagraha and ahimsa.

In response Gandhi said, "I felt that Indians residing in England ought to do their bit in the war." And ideally, he hoped his support of England would benefit India-England relationships. It wasn't long before nearly 80 Indian volunteers started first-aid training.

But as winter approached, Gandhi's health declined, and he became very ill with a respiratory disease called pleurisy. The damp, chilly weather of England worsened his condition, so something needed to change. Gandhi and Kasturba decided to return to the warmer climate of India.

A HERO'S WELCOME

After staying nearly five months in England, Gandhi and Kasturba arrived in Bombay at the start of 1915. They were surprised to learn that many people all across India viewed them as heroes with celebrity-like status. Many admired the work they had done on behalf of Indian rights in South Africa. Gandhi was often showered with praise, and people would frequently kneel to touch his feet in a gesture of respect. However, this adulation often made Gandhi feel uncomfortable.

Although Gokhale was still not feeling well, he had returned to Bombay to throw Gandhi and Kasturba an elaborate reception in their honor. With all the pomp and ceremony, Gandhi felt out of place at the posh party. While other guests wore fancy clothes and jewels, he was dressed in the simple cotton apparel of an indentured Indian with a turban, cloak, and loincloth worn around the waist. Unsuitable or not, these were the simple iconic clothes he would wear for the rest of his life.

Over the next few weeks, Gandhi had long conversations with Gokhale. Gandhi asked about joining the Servants of India Society, which Gokhale had founded in 1905 to fight for social reform and empower Indians against British rule. The society naturally appealed to Gandhi. Various members, however, didn't want Gandhi to join the group, saying his behavior was too radical.

Gokhale advised Gandhi to hold off on politics for a while and spend one year traveling around India to gain a better understanding of India and its people. For the next year, Gandhi did just that. He intentionally traveled third class on unkempt, crowded trains to better understand how Indians were treated. He journeyed all over India and visited many villages and cities. And he talked with people and learned about the serious problems and poverty facing the country.

THE ENCHANTING SHANTINIKETAN ASHRAM

Before Gandhi returned to India, various members of the Phoenix Settlement had already moved back to the country and were living at the Shantiniketan Ashram, located in West Bengal in northeastern India. Shantiniketan was a beautiful, peaceful world surrounded by lush greenery, rose gardens, and forests where deer roamed. At the time, nearly 125 students and teachers lived at the ashram. Residents worshipped in a nondenominational temple and studied or taught subjects such as art, music, dance, and literature. Classes were often held outdoors, and residents had opportunities to discuss heady subjects such as politics, as well as play music, practice yoga, and meditate.

After short visits to Rajkot and Porbandar to see relatives, Gandhi and Kasturba traveled to Shantiniketan, where they stayed for just a few days. Sadly, Gandhi learned Gokhale had died, and they promptly left the ashram to attend the leader's funeral in the city of Pune (also known as Poona). Gokhale's death was a great loss for Gandhi, but the loss also inspired him to carry on.

Gandhi and Kasturba were eager to settle down in India. Many cities were considered as sites for their next ashram, and Gandhi chose Ahmedabad, a large city in Gujarat. Gandhi liked the idea of returning to the state of Gujarat where he was born. In addition, Ahmedabad was also known for its textile industry and milled cloth, which complemented Gandhi's budding interest in the arts of spinning and weaving.

Rabindranath Tagore, Poet and Sage

Rabindranath Tagore was a famous Indian poet and sage (someone known for being wise or profound) who was the first non-European writer to win the Nobel Prize in Literature, which he was awarded in 1913. A Hindu, he was born in Kolkata (Calcutta), India, in 1861, eight years before Gandhi was born. He died in 1941. Tagore was considered a polymath, which is a great thinker who is knowledgeable in many subjects such as art, literature, and music. He founded Shantiniketan in 1901 as an experimental school and ashram, and he became well known for his literary works.

Tagore and Gandhi were devoted friends. Although they had very different personalities, they were both united in their love for India and dislike of British rule. While Gandhi expressed his desire for social reform through methods such as fasting, marching, and going to jail, Tagore

advocated for change through poetry and art. After Tagore wrote that Gandhi was a "Great Soul in peasant's garb," people started to call Gandhi "Mahatma," which means "great soul" or "saint." Some of Tagore's most famous poems include "Where the Mind Is Without Fear," "Freedom," and "Fireflies."

Rabindranath Tagore. *Wikimedia Commons*

Make a Meditation Mat

*Meditation is a practice of focusing the mind inward to reach a contemplative mental state some people find relaxing or spiritual. There are different ways to meditate, but a repeated **mantra**, such as saying "**om**," and taking deep breaths are common ways to help focus the mind. Gandhi practiced silent Mondays, not speaking the entire day. He also achieved a meditative state while spinning cotton on his spinning wheel, called a **charkha**. With fabric, foam, and hand stitching, you can make a unique and comfortable meditation mat.*

YOU'LL NEED

* ✳ Quilted fabric (1-inch diamond double-faced, 36 by 20 inches [91 by 51 cm])
* ✳ Tape measure
* ✳ Scissors
* ✳ Straight pins
* ✳ Thread, all-purpose
* ✳ Needle (medium)
* ✳ Foam insert, 1 by 15 by 17 inches (2.5 by 38 by 43 cm)
* ✳ 4 tassels
* ✳ Felt square, 9 by 12 inches (23 by 30 cm)
* ✳ Craft glue

1. Cut a 36-by-20-inch (91-by-51-cm) piece

A yogi meditating in a garden.
Wikimedia Commons PD-US

of fabric, fold the fabric over to form a boxy shape that is 18 by 20 inches (46 by 51 cm), and pin together along right and left sides.

2. Thread your needle, pull the thread down to the bottom, making a double thread, and knot the ends together; 36-inch (91-cm) lengths of thread work well. Now, stitch the right side of the folded fabric, leaving the top open. Stitch along the raw edges of the fabric, making small loop stitches about ¼ inch (.6 cm) apart. When you've used most of your thread, leave about 3 inches (8 cm) to knot your thread. Then, thread your needle with a new piece and start stitching again. Stitch the entire length of the right side *twice*, for a sturdy seam.

3. Repeat the same method to sew closed the left side of your fabric. Leave the top edge unstitched for now.

4. Once you've sewn your mat together on both sides, remove the pins, turn the fabric inside out, and flatten.

5. Insert the foam into the open end. Tuck under the open edges of fabric, and carefully close the seam with pins. With a small loop stitch as before, stitch together the folded end *twice*. Once you've stitched the opening closed, remove the pins. Smooth the mat with your hands and trim excess thread.

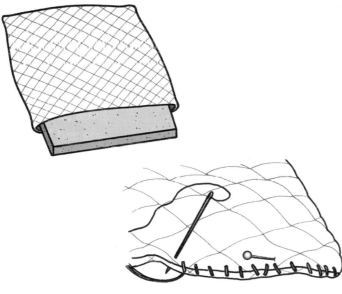

6. Now it's time to decorate your mat. Sew four small tassels to each corner. Trace the "om" symbol on this page to cut a pattern on a felt square. Glue the "om" symbol in the center of your mat.

7. Once your mat is finished, you might like to use it to try out meditation. Sit on your mat, keeping your back straight, and cross your legs. Now, for a few minutes, take deep breaths in and out, while focusing only on your breath.

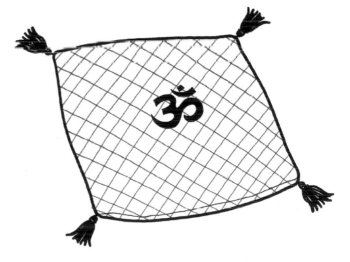

A main house at the Sabarmati Ashram.

Courtesy of Gandhi Heritage Portal

A NEW ASHRAM

In May 1915, Gandhi's family and members of the Phoenix Society settled into a new home named the Satyagraha Ashram located on the outskirts of Ahmedabad in the village of Kochrab. Here, residents dined in a common kitchen and lived as a family, complying with Gandhi's basic rules of eating a vegetarian diet, working with one's hands, farming, seeking truth, practicing nonviolence and ahimsa, and accepting untouchables into the ashram family. But when an untouchable family was invited to live at the ashram, some of the residents, including Kasturba, didn't like it. Kasturba found it hard to ignore age-old Hindu customs she had grown up with in India, and she worried her husband's reputation would suffer. Mohandas and Kasturba discussed the issue at length, and

eventually Kasturba came to accept the untouchable family.

Gandhi later moved his ashram to a larger site on the banks of the Sabarmati River, not far from the Sabarmati Central Jail. The Satyagraha Ashram was renamed the Sabarmati Ashram, and a building was constructed for spinning and weaving. Gandhi and Kasturba lived and worked at Sabarmati until 1933.

TRUE BLUE INDIGO

During Gandhi's first years back in India, he traveled the country searching for ways to help others. Sometimes people searched for him. In 1916, when Gandhi was about 47 years old, an Indian peasant farmer named Raj Kumar Shukla approached Gandhi and told him he needed help. His community was in trouble.

Raj Kumar was from the northern Champaran region of India in the state of Bihar near the Himalayan foothills. Champaran had prospered for years growing indigo plants to make blue-colored dye. But when a new synthetic indigo dye was manufactured, the market for the real indigo plant plummeted. Raj Kumar told Gandhi the poor indigo farmers of Champaran were often mistreated by British landlords, who charged them high farming fees and often beat and harassed them.

When Gandhi started to investigate the matter in Champaran, he was arrested and ordered to leave town. Local officials knew Gandhi was highly respected, so they chose not to jail him.

So when he was released, Gandhi didn't leave the town and he didn't give up. For more than six months he took up the plight of the impoverished indigo farmers and eventually succeeded in lowering their unfair farming fees. Kasturba also came to help the women and children with their homes, schools, and health care. In his autobiography, Gandhi wrote that "The ryots [farmers] who had all along remained crushed, now somewhat came to their own, and the superstition that the stain of indigo could never be washed out was exploded."

Given their success helping the village of Champaran, Gandhi and Kasturba realized that "India's problems could be solved after all—one district, one village, one afternoon, at a time."

FASTING FOR CHANGE

One of the effective techniques Gandhi used for social reform was fasting, which means going without food for days or weeks. As a child he had witnessed his mother, Putlibai, fast for religious reasons. He would nervously wait until she started eating again. As an adult, Gandhi used fasting to help change people's minds, to find solutions to problems, or for his own personal and spiritual reasons. Gandhi knew he was loved throughout India. He realized that Indians as well as the English would sit up and take notice when he was lying in bed wasting away from lack of food.

Gandhi's first fast in India occurred in 1918 in his efforts to fight for the poorly treated mill workers in Ahmedabad. The workers rightfully wanted more pay and better working conditions. Gandhi had friendly relations with the mill owners, so he stood in the middle between the owners and their workers.

Nonetheless, Gandhi encouraged the mill workers to go on strike, which they did. Thousands of strikers met with Gandhi on the bank of the Sabarmati River to discuss their next moves. But after two weeks, the agitated strikers seemed like they might become violent. This worried Gandhi because he wanted the strikers to be peaceful and nonviolent while fighting for their rights. An idea came to him—he would go on a fast until the strike was settled. After Gandhi fasted for three days, the strike was called off and a settlement was reached.

News quickly spread of Mahatma Gandhi's great work on behalf of India's poor. The same year, Gandhi also helped peasant farmers in the Kheda district near Ahmedabad achieve better treatment

Gandhi during a fast.
Getty, Keystone, Hulton Archive

from their employers. Gandhi's successful efforts on behalf of the indigo farmers in Champaran, the mill workers in Ahmedabad, and the peasant farmers in Kheda increased the activist's prominence and high regard in India. Through these efforts, Gandhi was often viewed as the "Mahatma" and mobbed by admiring crowds. He admitted he was more of a leader trying to be like a saint, rather than the other way around.

And he didn't always make popular decisions. In the spring of 1918, India's viceroy (a type of governor), Lord Chelmsford, asked Gandhi to help recruit Indians for World War I. Although contradictory to his beliefs on nonviolence, Gandhi hoped his recruitment efforts for England would be an act of goodwill and help pave the way for India's independence. But few Indians enlisted in the war effort, and his recruiting campaign was ineffective. World War I ended about six months later in November 1918.

A TERRIBLE TURN OF EVENTS

After the war ended, Gandhi continued to push for India's independence. He hoped for a peaceful transition with England and a positive partnership in the future. In 1919 he published a newspaper called *Young India* to reach Indian readers and to promote the country's fight for freedom. However, instead of giving India its much-desired independence, England turned the tables and passed the 1919 Rowlatt Act, which further restricted Indians' rights. The Rowlatt Act gave the British the right to jail Indian activists without a fair trial. Gandhi knew the act was highly unjust, and he came up with a plan to oppose it.

On April 6, 1919, Gandhi asked Indians throughout the country to take part in a national strike called a *hartal*, which would be a peaceful day of prayer and fasting during which no one would go to work or school. In essence, all of India would shut down. Unfortunately, the strike got out of hand in some areas: rioting occurred, property was destroyed, and people were killed.

Gandhi quickly realized India wasn't ready for this kind of peaceful, wide-scale protest. He soon called off the hartal, saying, "It was unbearable for me to find that the labourers, amongst whom I had spent a good deal of my time, whom I had served, and from whom I had expected better things, had taken part in the riots, and I felt I was a sharer in their guilt."

A PEACEFUL GATHERING TURNS DEADLY

The British military then sent General Reginald Dyer to take charge of the escalating violence. Dyer banned all gatherings in public places. His warning, however, did not reach everyone throughout the country.

That April, a large group of Indians met in the Jallianwala Bagh garden in the town of Amritsar to conduct a peaceful gathering. Dyer found out about the gathering and took his armed soldiers into the garden, which was enclosed by large walls. Dyer commanded his soldiers to shoot. Unable to escape, hundreds of unarmed men, women, and children were killed, and more than 1,000 were wounded. Out of desperation, people dove into a garden well to avoid being shot, and drowned.

Gandhi was shocked to learn that the peaceful gathering had turned deadly and innocent people had been ruthlessly killed. He gave back his ambulance corps medals of honor he had received from the British government. Something had to change.

REFUSING TO COOPERATE

Even though Gandhi disliked British rule, he had worked long and hard to show his loyalty to England. But like many, his opinion of the English plummeted after the tragic Jallianwala Bagh massacre in 1919.

Gandhi then became very involved in the Indian National Congress (INC), which was founded in 1885 as the largest Indian organization working toward the country's independence from England. Many people joined India's independence movement, including social reformer Annie Besant, who now lived in India. Besant helped launch the 1916 Indian Home Rule League, which advocated freedom from British rule. A year later, Besant became the first woman president of the INC. Although Gandhi and Besant did not always see eye to eye, both fought for India's freedom.

After the massacre, Gandhi knew it was time for India to take a new approach. Devastated and disheartened, Gandhi's feelings of loyalty to England changed forever at this time. He came up with a new form of satyagraha and called it "non-co-operation"

(noncooperation). He believed it was time for India to stop cooperating with England, whether it was working for the English or paying taxes.

One method of Gandhi's noncooperation movement was to boycott British products. Gandhi encouraged Indians to refuse to buy and wear foreign-made clothes. Instead, he wanted Indians to recapture their age-old traditions of spinning their own thread and weaving their own fabric. Making their own clothes would provide employment for many people throughout India in a positive and peaceful way. In his autobiography Gandhi wrote, "The object that we set before ourselves was to be able to clothe ourselves entirely in cloth manufactured by our own hands."

Gandhi started to spend a great deal of time spinning cotton at a spinning wheel. At times,

Gandhi at his spinning wheel.
Getty, Margaret Bourke-White, Masters Collection

Powerful Symbols

Gandhi's clothes and his longtime focus on spinning spoke volumes about his political and philosophical views. By wearing a traditional cotton loincloth, Gandhi aligned himself with the poor of India while also shunning European-style dress. In simple terms, Gandhi was demonstrating pride of his Indian heritage, thereby encouraging other Indians to feel the same.

By sitting on the floor and working for hours at a spinning wheel, Gandhi demonstrated the importance of taking matters into one's own hands rather than always relying on technology or mass production to get a job done. Cotton grows abundantly in India, and for centuries the country had been a major player in the textile industry, which provided employment for many Indians. With the Industrial Revolution, however, Indian cotton was shipped to England to be milled into cloth, which Indians had to then buy back. Gandhi encouraged Indians to make and wear clothes from India rather than buying fabric or garments manufactured outside the country.

These messages of self-sufficiency had a powerful effect on Indians, and Gandhi's spinning wheel became a symbol of India's independence from England.

Gandhi would ask people to take their foreign-made clothes and throw them in a large heap to be set on fire. Gandhi also encouraged Indians to stage nonviolent protests against British authorities. Millions of Indians followed his direction.

THE GREAT TRIAL

England responded to Gandhi's noncooperation movement by sending tens of thousands of Indians to jail. In 1922, however, Indians in the town of Chauri Chaura reacted with violence and brutally killed a group of policemen. Horrified to learn this, Gandhi called off all scheduled protests and began a five-day fast as a sacrifice for the killed policemen. He then pleaded with Indians to refrain from all violence toward British authorities.

The violence subsided, but there were serious consequences. One month after the Chauri Chaura killings, Gandhi was arrested and tried in court for inciting the violence. During his court case, which some called "The Great Trial," Gandhi stated he was never in favor of violence. But he pleaded guilty to his charges and said he would accept the most stringent punishment. Gandhi also used this time in the courtroom to give an impassioned speech about the severe and ongoing problems of British rule.

After listening to Gandhi's words, the presiding judge acknowledged Gandhi's patriotism and leadership. He then sentenced Gandhi to six years in the Yerwada Central Jail (also spelled as Yerawada or Yeravda) in Pune, India, for his acts against British authorities, specifically related to articles he wrote in *Young India*.

In jail, Gandhi was allowed to use a spinning wheel and to read books. He was also given paper and a pen, which enabled him to begin writing his autobiography. Before too long, however, Gandhi suffered acute appendicitis and was hospitalized. British authorities then released him from jail after two years of his six-year sentence.

GANDHI FASTS FOR UNITY

While Gandhi had been in jail, his Satyagraha movement had stalled throughout India. For years Gandhi had encouraged Hindu and Muslim harmony and unity in India. But while he was imprisoned, Hindus and Muslims had grown apart and started to fight. As a response, Gandhi went on a 21-day fast in 1924, which is often referred to as "The Great Fast." As the days went on, Gandhi became thinner, frail, and nauseous; he nearly died. When his fast was finally broken with a sip of orange juice, Hindu and Muslim relations improved for a time.

Over the next few years, Gandhi continued working for Indian rights but withdrew from the Indian National Congress. He wanted to shift his attention toward social reform issues. Deep down he knew India's independence depended on the country's ability to become strong, self-reliant, and unified. Gandhi traveled from village to village and encouraged Indians to spin cotton and weave it to make a natural cotton fabric called *khadi*. He also helped India's socially disadvantaged poor people and worked hard to improve the lives of untouchables. His popularity soared.

But there was a great deal of unrest in India, and violence was always on the horizon. To avoid more bloodshed, Gandhi became active in the Indian National Congress again in the late 1920s. At an INC meeting in Calcutta, members came up with an ultimatum for England: either get out of India by the end of 1929 or suffer the consequences of a national noncooperation movement. Gandhi knew something big needed to be done to push for independence. But it needed to be nonviolent and dramatic, and it needed to get the attention of the media. He looked to the sea for inspiration.

Spin Thread from a Cotton Boll

Cotton grows abundantly in the warm climate of India. Gandhi didn't like the fact that India's fabric industry had been taken over by European industrialists. He realized many Indians could benefit and earn wages by locally producing their own thread and weaving it into natural cotton fabric. He encouraged people throughout India to use charkhas to spin thread from cotton bolls. Discover how to pull and spin thread from the fluffy part of the cotton plant.

YOU'LL NEED

- ❋ Cotton boll (available online, or use 100% cotton balls)
- ❋ Chopstick
- ❋ Small potato

1. Hold a cotton boll plant with its husk and seeds intact. Pull apart the many cotton sections with seeds from the husk. How many sections are there?

2. Feel the seeds embedded in the cotton sections. Gently pull the cotton fibers away from the seeds so you can see the seeds.

3. Now, tug and pull out the seeds from the cotton boll sections in a process called ginning. How many seeds did you find? Was it difficult to pull out the seeds?

4. Carefully fluff apart one seedless cotton boll section to make it bigger and flatter. You can pat it together so it remains in one piece. How does it feel? What does it look like?

5. Now, hold the seedless cotton boll section (or a store-bought cotton ball) in one hand and use the thumb and index finger of your other hand to pinch a section of the cotton. Gently pull a piece of the cotton away from the section while slowly twisting it. A piece of thread will form. It sometimes helps to carefully roll the thread against the top of your thigh while slowly twisting it.

6. To continue making thread, make a simple spindle by pushing a chopstick into a small potato. Leave a 1-inch (2.5-cm) point at the spindle end.

7. Once you have about 3 inches (8 cm) of thread, wrap and tie it around your spindle near the potato. While still holding your cotton in one hand, hold the spindle upright in your other hand and continue to pull and spin thread from the cotton. This is where cotton thread originates. Many products such as shirts, towels, and sheets are made of 100 percent cotton. Look around your home and make a list of items made from 100 percent cotton, which is often indicated on a product's label.

Gandhi led marchers 240 miles from the Sabarmati Ashram to the coastal town of Dandi.

Getty, Mansell, The LIFE Picture Collection

MARCHING TOWARD INDEPENDENCE

To think that collecting a pinch of salt from the sea could help free India! —Arun Gandhi

Gandhi had an indomitable spirit and worked tirelessly to help India gain its independence from England. Even in his later years he marched for justice, traveled to London to meet with political leaders, endured many life-threatening fasts, and was imprisoned over and over again.

The year 1929 was a tense time for India. Jawaharlal Nehru, a longtime follower of Gandhi and a leader of India's independence movement, was now president of the Indian National Congress. The INC had given England an ultimatum to give India its rightful freedom or Indians would conduct more acts of civil disobedience and noncooperation against Britain. Like Nehru and many Indians throughout the country, Gandhi was fed up with England's continuing control of their homeland. Something needed to be done. When the last day of 1929 passed and England still had not granted India's freedom, Gandhi set into motion a plan that amazed the world.

SALT FOR JUSTICE

Gandhi was angry that the British government controlled one of India's basic resources and necessities for food—salt. India was surrounded by salty ocean waters, and salt was readily available from the ocean or from shallow salt pans typically located along the coast.

But the British would not allow Indians to collect, produce, or sell their own salt. Even if Indians lived near salt pans, they weren't allowed to extract any salt from them. According to imposed salt laws, Indians could only buy salt from the British. Plus, salt was heavily taxed, which made it difficult for Indians to afford it. If Indians were caught producing or selling salt, they could be sent to jail. Gandhi knew this was highly unfair and considered it a crime against India. He first wrote a letter to Lord Irwin, the viceroy of India at the time, to ask for the salt law to be abolished. When Lord Irwin responded negatively to his letter, Gandhi took action into his own hands in the form of a peaceful but powerful march of civil disobedience.

THE SALT MARCH

On March 12, 1930, 60-year-old Gandhi began his historic Salt March wearing sturdy sandals and carrying a long bamboo walking stick. Setting out from the Sabarmati Ashram, he led about 80 men and women on a 24-day, 240-mile trek due south to the seaside town of Dandi near the Arabian Sea. Gandhi's son Manilal, who lived in South Africa at the time, traveled back to India to join the march. In addition, an American journalist named Webb Miller joined in to report on the big event and let the world know what was happening.

As Gandhi and his followers walked from town to town, more and more Indians joined the march. Soon, thousands of people were walking with Gandhi. The march was a hot, dusty, and winding journey, covering about 12 miles a day. It was a mighty show of strength. Onlookers stood on the sidelines and showered the marchers with flowers, candy, and coins. Gandhi stopped in

Gandhi broke British law by scooping up a little salt.
Getty, ullstein bild collection

villages along the way to give speeches about the power of satyagraha and civil disobedience.

The marchers arrived in Dandi on April 5 and prayed and rested through the night. The next morning the group followed Gandhi to the ocean waters, where he took a dip in the sea. His next move was illegal. Gandhi knelt down and scooped up a small handful of salt from the mud of the Dandi beach, which meant he had just committed a crime by breaking the English salt laws. This simple and symbolic act of civil disobedience hit newspaper headlines around the world, awakening readers to the injustice in India.

Gandhi was hailed as a hero, and a wave of enthusiasm spread across the country. The Salt March ignited a campaign of mass civil disobedience. Gandhi invited Indians to collect and make their own salt and endure imprisonment if need be. Soon, Indians along the coastline were collecting pots and pans of seawater to make their own salt—thereby boldly defying British law. People in the cities started to buy Indian salt instead of British salt. It wasn't long before thousands of Indians were arrested and jailed, including Gandhi, who was imprisoned soon after his act of defiance.

Although Gandhi was in jail, his Salt March continued in full force. The third week in May, Indian poet Sarojini Naidu stepped up to lead the protest. She bravely led nearly 2,500 marchers to the Dharasana Salt Works, a British-controlled salt factory located about 25 miles south of Dandi. There, a peaceful protest was scheduled to take place.

Journalist Webb Miller was still reporting on the protest, which quickly turned ugly. Once the protesters broke the law at the Dharasana Salt Works by refusing to leave, British-led policemen were ready and waiting to respond. They used wooden batons with metal tips to brutally club hundreds of the marchers who, as Gandhi advised, did not fight back or even try to defend themselves. Blow after blow rained down on the Indian protesters' heads and backs.

The injured were treated at a temporary medical center. Manilal's skull was fractured during the protest, and he was taken to a prison hospital. Miller immediately sent out a news story about the harrowing event to stunned readers around the world.

WEBB MILLER UPI MAY 21, 1930
DHARASANA, INDIA NEWS STORY

The volunteers formed into columns, with their leaders carrying ropes and wire cutters. They advanced slowly for half a mile—a ghostly procession—toward the salt works.

The 400 police clutched their clubs and about 25 of them revealed their rifles as the volunteers approached. There were a few cheers and then the leaders who had ropes attempted to lasso the posts holding up the barbed wire, intending to uproot them. The police ran up and demanded that they disperse. The volunteers refused.

Police charged, swinging their clubs and belaboring the raiders on all sides. The volunteers

Evaporate Salt in the Tradition of Gandhi

When Gandhi took a pinch of salt from the sea during his historic Salt March, he broke the law. But he sent a loud and clear message for others to do the same. Indians who lived near coastlines went to beaches and collected seawater, from which they then extracted salt. For this activity, you'll use heat to turn salted tap water or—if you have access to the ocean—actual saltwater to salt. Note: the salt produced in this activity should be sampled only—not used as table salt.

ADULT SUPERVISION REQUIRED

OPTION #1: TAP WATER

YOU'LL NEED

- ❋ Oven
- ❋ Tap water, 1 cup
- ❋ Measuring cup
- ❋ Sea salt, from a store
- ❋ Tablespoon
- ❋ Spoon
- ❋ Glass baking dish, approximately 9 by 13 inches (23 by 33 cm)
- ❋ Hot pads
- ❋ Spatula
- ❋ Small bowl

1. Preheat oven to 350 degrees Fahrenheit.

2. Add 1 cup of tap water to measuring cup. Now, add 1 tablespoon of sea salt to the water and stir with the spoon. The water will become cloudy; wait about 15 minutes until the water is clear.

3. Pour the salted water into the baking dish. Carefully place the baking dish in the preheated oven for 30 minutes. After 30 minutes, turn off the oven and let the dish continue to dry inside the oven for 30 more minutes or until salt crystals have formed in the base of the dish. Check the baking dish about every 15 minutes to watch how the water changes and to make sure the salt does not brown or burn. Salt should turn white.

4. Use hot pads to remove the baking dish from the oven. Let it cool completely.

5. When the dish has cooled, use a spatula to scrape the salt from the dish. Place the salt in a small bowl.

6. Sample a small amount of salt. How does it taste? What is the texture like? How is it different from the original sea salt you used or from table salt?

OPTION #2: OCEAN WATER

YOU'LL NEED

* ❋ Oven
* ❋ Coffee filter, 4-ounce size
* ❋ Large glass, 16-ounce size
* ❋ Saltwater, 1½ cups from the ocean
* ❋ Saucepan, 2-quart size
* ❋ Stovetop
* ❋ Glass baking dish, approximately 9 by 13 inches (23 by 33 cm)
* ❋ Hot pads
* ❋ Spatula
* ❋ Small bowl

1. Preheat oven to 350 degrees Fahrenheit.

2. Dampen a coffee filter, and wrap it over the top of your glass. Holding the filter in place with one hand, pour 1½ cups of salt-water into the glass through the filter to remove any sediment.

3. Place the filtered saltwater in the sauce-pan on a stovetop; boil for about 1 minute and let cool.

4. Now, place 1 cup of filtered, boiled salt-water in the baking dish and follow steps 3 through 5 from option #1. Note: After you scrape the saltwater salt into a small bowl, sample a small amount. How does this salt taste? What is the texture like? How is it different from the salt you made from salted water or from table salt?

made no resistance. As the police swung hastily with their sticks, the natives simply dropped in their tracks.

Less than 100 yards away I could hear the dull impact of clubs against bodies. The watching crowds gasped, or sometimes cheered as the volunteers crumpled before the police without even raising their arms to ward off the blows. With almost unbelievable meekness they submitted to the clubbing and were carried away by their comrades who had collected a score of stretchers.

The world could now see the unjust and brutal treatment of Gandhi's disobedient but peaceful protesters. Many people were outraged.

Gandhi attended the second Round Table Conference in London.

Getty, Hulton Archive Collection, Imagno

A CHANGE OF MIND?

Gandhi's Salt March drew attention, and according to Mary and Mike Furbee's book *The Importance of Mohandas Gandhi*, "The British were deeply embarrassed by this widely publicized brutality that had been perpetrated by police officers under their control." Hoping to mend relations, the British government organized three Round Table Conferences from 1930 to 1932 among British politicians and Indian delegates. The conferences were held in London to discuss reforms for India. Gandhi did not attend the first conference in November 1930 because he was in jail.

The following January, however, Gandhi was freed from jail. Lord Irwin met with him to work on solving the escalating unrest in India and changing some of Britain's policies toward India. Over a series of eight meetings, the Gandhi-Irwin pact was drawn up in February 1931. This agreement stated that if Indians stopped their acts of civil disobedience, the many Indians who were jailed during the Salt March would be released. In addition, Indians who lived near the sea would be allowed to make and sell salt. However, the Gandhi-Irwin pact did not agree to India's independence. But Gandhi hoped it was a step in the right direction.

That August, Gandhi was invited to London to attend the second Round Table Conference with British leaders and Indian delegates to discuss the future of India. At the conference, Gandhi urged British leaders to grant India its independence. He also spent time in London as a goodwill ambassador, visiting unemployed mill workers and coal miners. He even met with English film actor Charlie Chaplin.

After the second Round Table Conference, Gandhi returned to India without good news. Nothing had changed. Gandhi continued to remain hopeful that India would achieve independence one day. But he was soon discouraged all over again. Lord Willingdon, the new viceroy for India, cracked down on the Indian National Congress, calling it an illegal organization. He arrested top INC leaders.

A FAST UNTO DEATH?

In 1932, Gandhi was once again sent to the Yerwada Jail for acts of civil disobedience. This time he was imprisoned with his trusted personal assistant, Mahadev Desai, who had worked closely with him since 1917 at the Sabarmati Ashram. In jail, Gandhi and Desai had two rituals. They would say morning prayers at 4:00 AM each day and then make a sweet beverage by pouring boiling water over lime or lemon juice and honey. Gandhi was said to cover this drink with a piece of cloth to keep out germs.

Gandhi also spent time in jail spinning cotton, meditating, reading, and keeping current with the news. He was shocked to learn that during the third Round Table Conference the British government supported a new Indian constitution to create separate electorate voting groups for Hindus, Muslims, Buddhists, **Sikhs**, Europeans, and untouchables. Bhimrao R. Ambedkar, an Indian

Bhimrao R. Ambedkar.
Wikimedia Commons

lawyer who fought for the rights of untouchables, was in favor of these separate electorates. He wanted untouchables to have a voice and not be left out of India's politics. But Gandhi disagreed and saw this political separation as divisive, discriminatory, and a way to stall the formation of a unified and independent India.

To oppose these voting measures and to protest the mistreatment of untouchables, whom Gandhi called Harijan ("children of God"), Gandhi began a fast in the Yerwada jail. From September 20, 1932, on, he would not eat one bite of food,

Speak Up for a Cause

When Gandhi looked around his community and discovered problems, he took action. Although he was a shy lawyer at first, he went on to become a powerful and influential speaker. Being able to express yourself through words takes practice, and it can be an effective way to create change. For this activity, write a speech about a cause you care about.

YOU'LL NEED

* ❋ Access to the Internet or a library
* ❋ Paper
* ❋ Pen or pencil

1. Think about situations in your community that could be improved. Are people without shelter? Is there enough food for everyone? Does everyone have access to medical care? Are some people's rights ignored or abused? Are your friends or family members being bullied?

2. Write down a list of possible topics and research the topics online, visit your local library, or talk with local leaders, community members, and family to learn more about these issues. Narrow down your topics and choose one cause you care deeply about.

3. Now, write a one- to two-page speech, with a beginning, middle, and end.

4. Start your speech with an introduction that grabs listeners' attention. You might begin with a personal anecdote you feel passionate about. Next, present important facts, statistics, and other information in the middle of your speech that help back up your message. Close your speech with a poignant thought or call to action.

5. Once you've written your speech, read it aloud and make revisions. When you are happy with your words, you might like to share your speech with friends, family, or community members.

even if it threatened his life, until there was a unified way for Hindus and Harijan to vote.

Like Gandhi, Ambedkar was a beloved leader in India. Ambedkar preferred to use the name **Dalit** for untouchables, which is a Sanskrit term meaning "oppressed." Ambedkar viewed Gandhi's fast as a manipulative stunt, and he considered the name Harijan to be offensive and demeaning to untouchables. Many Indians thought otherwise. With the news of Gandhi's fast and potential death, a panic erupted throughout the country. The idea that their Mahatma would perish was unthinkable. According to Catherine Bush in her book, *Mohandas Gandhi*, there were "frantic negotiations between India and London to rework the proposed constitution."

After six days, Gandhi's health deteriorated and he looked limp lying on his prison cot. Finally, when a plan called the Poona Pact was agreed upon for a single Hindu electorate, Gandhi broke his fast. Although Gandhi's fast did not instantly change ancient prejudice against untouchables, it shed light on the injustice of treating untouchables in such a negative way. In 1933, Gandhi published a weekly newspaper called *Harijan*.

After Gandhi was released from the Yerwada jail, he made big changes in his life, which was increasingly at risk. Some people strongly disagreed with his views and seemed determined to assassinate him. In June 1934, Gandhi and Kasturba were traveling in a motorcade in Pune, India, where Gandhi was scheduled to give a speech at a local auditorium. A bomb was hurled at one of the cars and injured seven individuals, including policemen. Fortunately, Gandhi and Kasturba were not injured.

A NEW ASHRAM

In 1936, Gandhi set up a new ashram in the quiet, small village of Segaon in central India near the city of Wardha. It was a very remote and rural setting, and there were few amenities. The village was about five miles from the nearest train station and did not have stores or a post office. Days could be very hot, and snakes and scorpions were common.

Gandhi constructed a simple mud and bamboo hut with a tile roof as his primary residence. In time, as more people arrived, huts, water wells, gardens for food, and classrooms were built to accommodate the growing community of family and followers. A new self-sufficient ashram had taken form. Gandhi named the ashram "Sevagram," which means, "village of service." Days would be spent in daily prayers, meditation, exercise, reading, writing, farming, chores, spinning cotton, schoolwork, preparing foods, and communal dining. Gandhi would continue to work on Indian rights from his new home at Sevagram, his primary home for the last 12 years of his life.

While at Sevagram, Gandhi knew a crisis in Europe was brewing over the horrifying actions of Adolph Hitler, the leader of Germany and the Nazi party. For the sake of humanity and to potentially thwart war, a number of Gandhi's associates asked him to write a letter to the German leader. Gandhi was a "strong critic of Nazi Germany" and

Gandhi started a new ashram in India called Sevagram, which means "village of service." *Courtesy of Gandhi Heritage Portal*

Gandhi's fifth grandson, Arun Gandhi, visited Gandhi at Sevagram Ashram when he was 12 years old. *Courtesy of Arun Gandhi*

felt reluctant to correspond with Hitler. But on July 23, 1939, he wrote a short letter to him saying, "It is quite clear that you are today the one person in the world who can prevent a war which may reduce humanity to the savage state. . . . Will you listen to the appeal of one who has deliberately shunned the method of war not without considerable success?"

Gandhi never heard back from Hitler. And just a few weeks later, World War II broke out when Germany invaded Poland on September 1, 1939, and England and France declared war on Germany two days later. The Second World War lasted six years, from 1939 until 1945, and millions of lives were lost.

Gandhi was discouraged that violence could occur on such a global scale with this new war. He cried when he imagined cherished places in London, such as Westminster Abbey, being destroyed. And even though England had been in the gradual process of giving India more and more independence, the war changed everything.

At the start of World War II, India's new British viceroy, Lord Linlithgow, announced India was going to side with England and its allies of France and Poland to fight against Germany and its allies of Italy and Japan. But the viceroy had not asked leaders of the Indian National Congress whether they wanted to participate in the war or not. This angered Gandhi and set into motion renewed plans for civil disobedience.

Faced with the potential of more violence in India, some British politicians wanted to grant India its independence right away. Other politi-

Gandhi's Grandson Remembers

Arun Gandhi is Manilal Gandhi's son, and Gandhi's fifth grandson. Arun was born in 1934 on the Phoenix Ashram near Durban, South Africa, and grew up during discriminatory apartheid. In 1946, when Arun was 12 years old, he was beaten by both white and black South Africans who thought his skin was either too dark or too light. Arun felt angry and frustrated. To help him, Arun's parents sent him to live with his grandfather at the Sevagram Ashram in India for two years.

It was a time of great personal growth and change for Arun. Later in life, he became a newspaper reporter for the *Times of India*, where he worked for 30 years. In 1987, Arun and his wife, Sunanda, moved to the United States and founded the M.K. Gandhi Institute for Nonviolence, now located in Rochester, New York. The couple devoted their lives to nonviolence, education, and helping the poor.

In October 2014, Arun Gandhi kindly responded to the following questions about his childhood.

What did you enjoy about growing up in South Africa?
There were very good moments, especially at the ashram Grandfather started. I played with African kids and had very good relationships with them. We used to collect old matchboxes and discarded buttons and make mini cars. We also collected old bicycle wheel rims and pushed them along with a stick. We had races and all kinds of wonderful games. We also had a stream running on the border of Phoenix Ashram, and the soil in the stream was black clay. We would dig up clay to make animal and human figurines. That kind of inventiveness was encouraged by my parents.

What was it like growing up during apartheid?
It was a very bitter experience because that was the time when apartheid was at its worst. There seemed to be a lot of hate everywhere, and it was not just directed to Indians or Africans. It seemed like everybody hated everybody else.

How was Sevagram Ashram helpful?
The first lesson Grandfather taught me was about understanding anger and being able to channel that energy into constructive action—instead of abusing it. He said anger is like electricity. It's just as useful and just as powerful if it is used intelligently. But it can be just as deadly and destructive if we abuse it.

How was Sevagram different from the Phoenix Ashram?
Phoenix was very beautiful. It was hilly, very green and fertile with beautiful trees and flowers. At Sevagram it was just the opposite. It was flat land, almost desert—dry and very hot and dusty with not too much greenery. But I had lots of friends, and during playtime we used to play soccer. We enjoyed simple outdoor games.

Describe a typical day at Sevagram.
I had a plan for the whole day from the time I got up to the time I went to bed. Grandfather said, "Time is too precious to be wasted." When I got up, I did my exercises and interfaith prayers. We prayed Muslim, Christian, Hindu, and Buddhist prayers. We all sat out in the open and prayed together. It was a unique experience.

Did you meditate?
Meditation was in the form of spinning cotton on the wheel. I used to spin very often with Grandfather. He spent one hour with me every day. He would explain things to me and help me with my lessons or tell me stories. Grandfather was a multitasker.

What did your grandfather teach you about getting along with others?
He taught me hate is not the right thing and we need to love and respect each other. He said relationships between people must be based on the four principles of respect, understanding, acceptance, and appreciation.

cians, such as Britain's prime minister, Winston Churchill, vehemently opposed the idea. The struggles for India's independence seemed never-ending and the world was in chaos. What would happen next?

QUIT INDIA!

On August 8, 1942, the Indian National Congress passed a resolution called "Quit India," telling England it was time to get out of India. Gandhi was at the forefront of this movement launched nearly three years after the start of World War II. The resolution stated that if England did not withdraw from India, a national campaign of civil disobedience and noncooperation would begin immediately.

After this bold call to action, Gandhi, Nehru, and INC leaders were promptly arrested, launching violent and deadly protests in India. Angry crowds tore up train tracks and set government buildings on fire, and many people were injured or killed. Gandhi and his devoted personal assistant Mahadev Desai were imprisoned at the Aga Khan Palace. The palace was located near the Mula River in Pune, India, and had been converted into a prison.

A few days later, Kasturba was also jailed at the palace for bravely announcing she would deliver a speech on behalf of her husband. Both Gandhi and Kasturba were now 73 years old. Although the prison was a stately looking palace, Gandhi and the others were watched over by guards and treated as prisoners.

During nearly two years under house arrest at the Aga Khan Palace, Gandhi was confronted with a great deal of personal loss and sadness. Only one week after their arrest, 50-year-old Mahadev Desai died from a heart attack. Desai had worked very closely with Gandhi for more than 20 years, and his death grieved Gandhi. Next, Kasturba's health started to fail and she developed bronchitis. Sadly, Kasturba died in Gandhi's arms on February 22, 1944, while still imprisoned. After wedding as young teens, the couple had remained married for more than 60 years.

A few months after Kasturba's death, Gandhi, now 75 years old, became very ill with malaria and was then released from the Aga Khan Palace. He was never imprisoned again.

INDEPENDENCE AT MIDNIGHT

Freedom for India was a slow, painful process that spanned many years and touched many lives. It didn't happen the way Gandhi hoped. But it did happen.

After World War II ended in 1945, Clement Attlee, a British politician, replaced Winston Churchill as the new prime minister of England. Attlee was a liberal politician, and unlike Churchill, he pushed for India's independence. In early 1947, Attlee appointed Lord Mountbatten, a naval officer and British statesman, as the new and final viceroy of India. Mountbatten soon scheduled what many believed was a rushed August 15, 1947, deadline for India's freedom from British rule. Mountbatten wanted to establish positive relations with Jawaharlal Nehru, Gandhi, and Muhammad Ali Jinnah, the leader of the Muslim League in India. But there were serious issues to sort out among Hindus, Sikhs, and Muslims in India.

As independence loomed on the horizon, Jinnah feared India's Hindu majority would take control of the country once it became free from England. He wanted Muslims to have a completely separate country as an independent homeland, so that Muslims would live in Pakistan—and Hindus and Sikhs would live in India.

As a way to reinforce the desire to create a separate Muslim state in Pakistan, the Muslim League announced an event called Direct Action Day to be held on August 16, 1946. However, the day set off fighting among Muslims, Hindus, and Sikhs in the city of Calcutta (now known as Kolkata) and spread to other regions in India. This violence set in motion the eventual partition of India. Mountbatten and a number of Indian leaders reluctantly agreed to move toward the India and Pakistan separation, and important steps in this direction happened about one year later.

On July 18, 1947, England enacted the Indian Independence Act 1947 that declared British India would be divided into the two countries of India and Pakistan. The official days of independence for the two countries would occur about one

(left) The Muslim League. Jinnah is seated in first row, fifth from right.
Wikimedia Commons, The British Library

(right) Lord Mountbatten.
Wikimedia Commons, United Kingdom Government

month later in mid-August. Gandhi was heartbroken over the concept of dividing India in this way. He feared the partition would only cause more problems, hostility, and suffering.

As the August deadline neared, Hindu, Sikh, and Muslim leaders pushed for nonviolence. But violence broke out nonetheless. Gandhi traveled to parts of India where bloodshed was severe and called for peace among Hindus, Sikhs, and Muslims.

With partition, millions of Indians were required to pack up and move. Hindus and Sikhs moved from Pakistan to India, and Muslims moved from India to Pakistan. Millions left their homes and communities behind. Many Hindus and Muslims who had lived side by side for generations felt frightened, uprooted, and displaced. Men, women, and children walked many miles each day without much food, water, or medical care en route to their new lives. After carrying heavy luggage for days, they would often leave it by the roadside to lighten the load. Some refugees traveled in cramped trains that were susceptible to attack. The displaced people made their new homes in crowded refugee camps.

As Gandhi suspected, the two-country partition was a divisive, traumatic, and deadly process. Brutal fighting and riots occurred, and some one million lives were lost.

The Partition of India

At the stroke of midnight on August 15, 1947, independence was declared for India. British rule had finally ended, and with it, India became the two separate countries of India and Pakistan. Pakistan was further divided into West Pakistan in northwest India, and East Pakistan in northeast India, which became Bangladesh in 1971. Leadership was needed for the two countries. Muhammad Ali Jinnah became the governor-general of Pakistan, and Jawaharlal Nehru became the prime minister of India.

Because the time for independence fell directly at midnight, Pakistan observed its independence on August 14, 1947, and India observed its independence on August 15, 1947. These dates for independence continue today.

MILLIONS MOURN

In 1948, Gandhi traveled to strife-torn Delhi. The violence was intense in the city, and Gandhi was there to help both Hindus and Muslims. He stayed in a friend's home called the Birla House in New Delhi, a district of Delhi. Even though Gandhi was elderly and somewhat frail by now, he fasted to help end violence and bring about peace. A number of historians believe this fast helped thwart a potential civil war in India. But there were Hindus who didn't like Gandhi's support of Muslims, and some Muslims saw Gandhi as the enemy.

Gandhi knew his life was in danger. Toward the end of January, a bomb exploded at an evening prayer service at the Birla House. Gandhi then had police stationed at points throughout the house and grounds. One radical Hindu named Nathuram

Godse was intent on assassinating Gandhi. At an evening prayer service on January 30, 1948, Godse walked straight up to Gandhi, bowed, and then pulled out a pistol and shot him three times in the chest. The great leader was killed instantly. Godse and his coconspirators were later convicted and punished for the crime.

On the day Gandhi was killed, Prime Minister Nehru gave a spontaneous radio speech and expressed his deep sadness, felt by many people in India and around the world. Comparing Gandhi to a great light, Nehru offered words of hope, saying in part, "The light that has illumined this country for these many years will illumine this country for many more years, and a thousand years later that light will still be seen in this country, and the world will see it and it will give solace to innumerable hearts."

Gandhi's funeral ceremony was held on January 31, 1948, in New Delhi, on the banks of the Yamuna River. It was a sad and difficult day for countless people all over the world. In Hindu tradition, Gandhi was cremated at the Raj Ghat memorial site on the Yamuna River. On that day, more than one million people walked together in unity to honor the courageous soul who had worked so hard to help India achieve its freedom.

Many people walked through the streets of Delhi in a memorial procession to honor the loss of Mahatma Gandhi.

Getty, Margaret Bourke-White, The LIFE Picture Collection

Nelson Mandela, president of South Africa, with members of the Congressional Black Caucus at an event at the Library of Congress, 1994.

Library of Congress LC-DIG-ppmsca-38881

GANDHI'S LEGACY

This is what my soul is telling me: be peaceful and love everyone. —Malala Yousafzai

Gandhi had many important roles in his lifetime. He was a student, lawyer, teacher, activist, social reformer, political and spiritual leader, son, husband, father, and grandfather. Whether it was where he lived, how he thought, or what he did, Gandhi spent his lifetime on a dedicated quest for truth, love, and God. He had the ability to see the good in people, befriend the enemy, and love humanity as a whole even when he encountered negativity and violence. Gandhi's life was a profound message of non-violence, unity, and peace. Many people kindly refer to him as "Gandhiji" to convey respect.

Gandhi led a simple yet powerful life. But it wasn't always that way. At the start of his career he wore finely tailored clothes, stayed in grand hotels, lived in stately homes, and earned a high salary. But Gandhi's values changed after he was treated poorly by people who felt superior to him, and after he witnessed others being abused. His eyes opened to discrimination, injustice, and the inequity between the haves and the have-nots. Gandhi began to simplify his life and turned toward helping Indians in need. His daily life revolved around prayer time, service to others, work, and reading. When he died, Gandhi had only a few possessions to his name, including his homespun clothes, glasses, sandals, watch, spinning wheel, eating bowl, and writing materials.

GANDHI'S INFLUENCE LIVES ON

The world continues to honor and recognize Mohandas Karamchand Gandhi with many books, articles, films, television shows, websites, photographs, and artwork—as well as statues, memorials, monuments, exhibits, peace organizations, and celebrations. People can visit Gandhi's ashrams in India and South Africa for a glimpse of where Gandhi lived and worked.

Gandhi's influence lives on today through the work of many individuals. The following leaders have courageously helped change the world through nonviolence. Like Gandhi, many of these freedom fighters have fought against injustice and dedicated their lives to helping others. Some have nonviolently courted arrest as a method for change, and they have all been recognized throughout the world for their dedication to peace and freedom.

NELSON ROLIHLAHLA MANDELA

Born in 1918, four years after Gandhi left South Africa, Rolihlahla Mandela was renamed Nelson Mandela by his schoolteacher, Miss Mdingane. Nelson grew up in the beautiful rolling hills of the Transkei region of eastern South Africa. His father was a leader of their Madiba clan, and his home was a *rondavel* with a thatched roof and mud floor. Nelson felt free to explore the wide-open spaces of his Qunu village in the Transkei—to run in the fields, ride oxen, and fish and swim in the nearby stream.

As a young adult, he studied at the University of Fort Hare and eventually became a lawyer. Mandela's life changed when he moved to Johannesburg and first witnessed apartheid, the legalized racial discrimination of whites against blacks. Determined to fight for equal rights of South African blacks, he joined the African National Congress in 1944 when he was 26. At first Mandela used Gandhi's nonviolent methods to promote

Gandhi on the beach with one of his grandchildren.
Getty, Keystone-France

Create a Community Peace Prize

Gandhi was nominated for a Nobel Peace Prize five times, but he was never awarded the prize. Named after Swedish industrialist Alfred Nobel, the Nobel Prizes are annual international awards for Chemistry, Economic Sciences, Literature, Medicine, Peace, and Physics. For this activity, come up with your own community peace prize you could give to a family member, friend, classmate, teacher, coach, or community member.

YOU'LL NEED

* Pencil
* Card stock, 8 ½ by 11 inches (21.5 by 28 cm)
* Scissors
* Markers
* Paper punch
* Ribbon

1. Think about acts of kindness or peace that others have taken that are deserving of recognition. Did a family member show courage in a situation? Did a friend help stop bullying? Did someone at your school or in your community help another in need?

2. Come up with a name for your peace prize.

3. Now, sketch a design of your peace prize medallion on your card stock. Use markers to add color, and then cut it out. Make a hole at the top with a paper punch, and hang your medallion from a ribbon.

4. Give your peace prize to someone of your choice.

change. Later, he chose more aggressive methods to end apartheid. Mandela was eventually imprisoned for 27 years, separating him from his wife and children. His imprisonment brought international attention to the antiapartheid movement in South Africa.

Mandela was released from prison in 1990, and he continued to fight against apartheid, stressing the importance of nonviolence, peace, and freedom. In 1993, he won the Nobel Peace Prize with Frederik Willem de Klerk, the South African president from 1989 to 1994, for their peaceful end of apartheid and their steps toward a new democratic South Africa. In 1994, Mandela was inaugurated as South Africa's first democratically elected president. Nelson Mandela died in 2013 at the age of 95, leaving a powerful legacy of one man's inspiring work and sacrifice for the rights and dignity of others.

MARTIN LUTHER KING JR.

When civil rights leader Martin Luther King Jr. was born in Atlanta, Georgia, in 1929, Gandhi was 60 years old. Martin grew up during the Great Depression in the United States and saw suffering from unemployment and poverty. As a boy, Martin first heard about Gandhi and the concepts of nonviolent protest from family friend Howard Thurman, a theologian and civil rights leader who had visited Gandhi in India in 1935.

Wanting to become a Baptist minister to be of service to others, King earned his bachelor of divinity degree from Crozer Theological Seminary in Pennsylvania in 1951, and his doctorate in systematic theology from Boston University in 1955. In 1954, King became a pastor at the Dexter Avenue Baptist Church in Montgomery, Alabama, which ignited his involvement in America's civil rights movement. King was a key figure in Montgomery's bus boycott, when African Americans Claudette Colvin and Rosa Parks were arrested for refusing to give up their bus seats to whites.

In 1959, when King was 30 years old, he traveled to India for a month-long visit. He had the

Martin Luther King Jr., 1967.
Library of Congress
LC-USZ62-111165

opportunity to meet with key Indian leaders, including Prime Minister Jawaharlal Nehru. After returning from India, he wrote an article for *Ebony* magazine titled "My Trip to the Land of Gandhi," and wrote, "While the Montgomery boycott was going on, India's Gandhi was the guiding light of our technique of non-violent social change." King's visit to India reinforced his commitment to nonviolence and civil rights in the United States; his forms of protest included boycotts, sit-ins, marches, and going to jail to create change.

In 1964 Martin Luther King Jr. received the Nobel Peace Prize for his work as a civil rights leader. Four years after receiving the award, King was assassinated in Memphis, Tennessee, on April 4, 1968, while helping to organize a march on behalf of the town's sanitation workers.

THE 14TH DALAI LAMA, TENZIN GYATSO

Gandhi was nearly 66 years old when a boy named Lhamo Thondup was born in the small farming hamlet of Takster, Tibet, in 1935. When Lhamo was only two years old, Tibetan officials recognized him as the 14th Dalai Lama, which is a holy title for the top spiritual leader of Tibetan Buddhism.

At age two, Lhamo was separated from his parents and home and taken to live in the Kumbum Monastery located miles away. Fortunately, a kindhearted monk looked after Lhamo. Over the next few years, the Thondup family was reunited with their young son in the city of Lhasa, the

The 14th Dalai Lama, 2006.
Wikimedia Commons, Creative Commons, Yancho Sabev

capital of Tibet. When Lhamo was five years old, he was officially proclaimed the 14th Dalai Lama and given the new name of Tenzin Gyatso. He then started his education at the Potala Palace in Lhasa. He studied reading, writing, poetry, meditation, debate, Tibetan art and culture, medicine, and Buddhist philosophy.

In 1950, Tibet was occupied by Communist China, which ended a long period of Tibetan self-rule. In response, 15-year-old Tenzin Gyatso became the political and spiritual leader for millions of Tibetan people. In 1959 China became more aggressive toward the Tibetan people and destroyed monasteries and used Tibetans as forced laborers. Advised to leave, the Dalai Lama secretly sought exile in Dharamsala, India, where he was received with respect and reverence.

Observing Peace and Kindness

Many important days are celebrated around the world to honor peace and nonviolence.

Gandhi Jayanti is a national holiday in India to honor the life and work of Gandhi, celebrated on October 2, Gandhi's birthday. The term *jayanti* means "jubilee." Many commemorative ceremonies, festivities, and prayer services pay tribute to Gandhi and nonviolence. On this day, political leaders often visit Raj Ghat, Gandhi's memorial in New Delhi. One of Gandhi's favorite devotional songs, titled "Raghupati Raghav," is often heard.

The **International Day of Nonviolence** is observed on October 2 every year around the world. The United Nations General Assembly, headquartered in New York City, first voted to establish this day in 2007 to promote messages of nonviolence throughout the world. The day is observed through many events and activities. For more information, see http://www.un.org/en/events/nonviolenceday/index.shtml.

The **International Day of Peace** is observed every year on September 21 around the world. The day was established in 1981 by the United Nations General Assembly and first observed in 1982. On this day of peace, the United Nations invites all countries around the world to cease all fighting, hostilities, and violence to observe peace through a variety of events and activities. For more information, see http://www.un.org/en/events/peaceday/.

National Bullying Prevention Month is observed in the United States every year for the month of October. National Bullying Prevention Month was founded in 2006 by the PACER (Parent Advocacy Coalition for Educational Rights) organization in Bloomington, Minnesota. PACER's National Bullying Prevention Center offers many anti-bullying programs and resources. For more information, see http://www.pacer.org/bullying/nbpm/.

The Dalai Lama continues to live in Dharamsala today and works on behalf of the Tibetan people. He also travels the globe to speak about nonviolence, the environment, compassion, joy, and world peace. A bestselling author of more than 100 books, the Dalai Lama is regarded as a man of peace.

In 1989, Tenzin Gyatso was awarded the Nobel Peace Prize for his commitment to nonviolence in freeing Tibet. In his acceptance speech for the Nobel, the Dalai Lama said, "I accept it as a tribute to the man who founded the modern tradition of non-violent action for change—Mahatma Gandhi—whose life taught and inspired me."

AUNG SAN SUU KYI

Aung San Suu Kyi was born in Rangoon, Burma (now known as Yangon, Myanmar), in 1945. Like India, Burma was also struggling to obtain independence from British rule. Suu Kyi's heroic father, Aung San, helped Burma gain its independence. Sadly, Suu Kyi's father was assassinated by military rivals when she was two years old. Her mother, Khin Kyi, became Burma's ambassador to India in 1960, and Suu Kyi grew up learning about Gandhi and his nonviolence movement. At 19, she traveled to England to study at St. Hugh's College of Oxford University, where she met Michael Aris, a British scholar of Tibetan culture. The couple married and had two sons, Alexander and Kim.

In 1988 Suu Kyi returned to Rangoon to take care of her dying mother. Burma had been under an oppressive one-party military regime since

1962, and many people approached Suu Kyi to help Burma become a free democracy. Suu Kyi gave an inspiring and empowering speech before a large crowd in the city and impressed many people as a future leader. Over the following months, Suu Kyi traveled throughout Burma and spoke to the Burmese people about democracy, freedom, and human rights. However, the military regime didn't like her prodemocracy efforts, and there were attempts to kill her.

In 1989, the military government renamed Burma "Myanmar." The following year, Suu Kyi founded the National League for Democracy (NLD) political party in Burma. The party won a landslide victory in national elections. In response, the Myanmar government did not recognize the NLD victory and placed Suu Kyi under house arrest, separating her from her husband and children.

In 1991, Aung San Suu Kyi was awarded the Nobel Peace Prize for her nonviolent resistance to Myanmar's military government. Still under house arrest, she was unable to accept the award in person, and her 18-year-old son, Alexander, delivered her acceptance speech. Suu Kyi was freed in 1995, but she was again placed under house arrest from 2000 to 2010. In total, she was incarcerated for nearly 15 years, separated from loved ones. She sacrificed her own freedom for the freedom of others.

In the country's 2015 elections, Suu Kyi's National League for Democracy claimed a historic victory in parliament, paving the way for a democratic government.

Aung San Suu Kyi, 2013.
Wikimedia Commons, Creative Commons, Claude TRUONG-NGOC

MALALA YOUSAFZAI

Malala Yousafzai was 15 years old when she was shot in the head by a Taliban gunman in 2012. Malala had been speaking out about the importance of girls being able to get an education in her country. It nearly cost her her life.

Malala was born in 1997 in Mingora, Pakistan, in the lush mountainous region of Swat Valley, sometimes called the "land of waterfalls." When the Taliban occupied Swat Valley, Malala felt like she was living in a war zone. Although she felt afraid at times, she continued attending school. In 2009, when Malala was 12, she started writing an anonymous blog for the British Broadcasting Corporation (BBC), expressing her thoughts about life and school in Swat as the Taliban clamped down on girls' freedoms to attend school, listen to music, watch television, or shop. Although she stopped writing the blog, her identity was revealed, and threats were made on her life.

One afternoon in 2012, a masked gunman jumped onto Malala's school van and shot her and two girls seated by her. Malala was rushed to a

Malala Yousafzai.
Getty, Chip Somodevilla

military hospital in Pakistan and then airlifted to England for multiple surgeries and rehabilitation. She and her two friends survived the attack.

The young girl's bravery and steadfast activism touched the hearts and minds of many as more people heard Malala's inspiring story. She continued to live in England and attend school. Malala became an international symbol of hope, peace, and education for millions of girls around the world.

In April 2013, Malala's portrait was featured on the cover of *Time* magazine as one of the 100 most influential people in the world, along with Aung San Suu Kyi. On her July 12 birthday in 2013, Malala spoke at the United Nations Youth Assembly in New York City and delivered a speech about the importance of education for people around the world. That October, the European Parliament awarded 16-year-old Malala the Sakharov Prize for Freedom of Thought. She also traveled to the White House to meet President Obama and his family.

In 2014, when Malala Yousafzai was 17 years old, she was awarded the Nobel Peace Prize, making her the youngest Nobel laureate yet. Malala shared the Nobel with Indian Kailash Satyarthi, and both were honored for their work championing young people's rights, including the right to an education.

Organize an Inspiring Film Fest

Films often help us learn more about issues in our world that need improvement. Through stories we can better understand another person's point of view, challenges, and successes. Invite friends or family over for an inspiring film fest.

YOU'LL NEED

* Films
* Room to present films
* Television with DVD or Blu-ray player

1. Figure out your "5 Ws"—**W**ho will attend, **W**hat movies will be shown, **W**hen your event will happen, **W**here you'll show the movies, and **W**hy you'd like to do this.

2. Select films you'd like to present and review your choices with a parent or adult before the event. Five films to consider include:

   Gandhi brings to light Gandhi's life as a lawyer in South Africa and his courageous fight for India's independence. Rated PG, this biopic stars Ben Kingsley as Gandhi. 190 minutes.

   Invictus is an inspiring film about President Nelson Mandela and his support of his country's national rugby team in post-apartheid South Africa. Rated PG-13, the film stars Morgan Freeman and Matt Damon. 133 minutes.

   He Named Me Malala is an inspirational true story that documents the life and journey of Malala Yousafzai, who risked her life to fight for children's rights. Rated PG-13, the documentary features Malala Yousafzai, Ziauddin Yousafzai, and Toor Pekai Yousafzai. 88 minutes.

   Norma Rae tells the riveting story of one woman's brave efforts to unite her coworkers to fight for better wages, workers' rights, and respect in the textile mill where she works. Rated PG, the film stars Sally Field and Beau Bridges. 110 minutes.

   Selma presents the dramatic 1965 civil rights march from Selma to Montgomery, Alabama, led by Martin Luther King Jr. to protest for African American voting rights. Rated PG-13, the film stars David Oyelowo and Carmen Ejogo. 128 minutes.

3. Invite your guests. After a movie is over, have a discussion so everyone will have a chance to talk about what they liked, didn't like, or learned about the story.

ACKNOWLEDGMENTS

I had seen the movie *Gandhi* and read some very interesting books about his life. Like many people, I have great respect and admiration for this inimitable leader. But there was a great deal I needed to learn about Gandhi's life, and more than two years of research and writing followed. I'm very grateful for the help of many individuals around the world, including Dr. Loriliai Biernacki, Lily Cook-Durland, Arun Gandhi (Gandhi's fifth grandson), Dorian Leveque, Bailey Lindgren, Mackenzie Matt, Michael McInneshin, Kit Miller, Priyanka Nayar, Caitlin Oriel, Dr. Joanne Punzo Waghorne, Katie Wisc, and Sally Wood. I'm also very appreciative of the help from Ms. Kinnari Bhatt and Dr. Tridip Suhrud for their guidance, and in providing so many historic photos for the book, courtesy of the Gandhi Heritage Portal, developed and maintained by the Sabarmati Ashram Preservation and Memorial Trust. In addition, I'm thankful for the generous help of the Navajivan Trust, Paramacharya Sadasivanathaswami with the Himalayan Academy in Hawaii and Plum Village. I would also like to thank my publisher Cynthia Sherry, my excellent editors Lisa Reardon and Ellen Hornor, designers Monica Baziuk and Sarah Olson, illustrator James Spence, my copyeditor Claudia Wood, and the many talented individuals at Chicago Review Press whose dedication and expertise helped make this book a reality.

PRONUNCIATION GUIDE

Arun (A-ROON)

Aung San Suu Kyi (oun-sahn-su-CHEE)

Bhimrao Ramji Ambedkar
    (BIM-ray RAM-jee AM-be-car)

Chhaganlal (CHA-gan-lal)

Dalai Lama (DA-lee LA-ma)

Devdas (DEV-des)

Gandhi (GAN-dee)

Gandhiji (GAN-di-gee)

Harilal (HAR-ee-lel)

Jawaharlal Nehru
    (ja-wah-HAR-lal NEH-ha-ru)

Jayanti (juy-UN-tee)

Karamchand (kar-UM-chand)

Karsandas (kar-SAN-das)

Kastur Kapadia
    (KAS-ter kuh-PAY-dee-yah)

Kasturba (kas-TER-ba)

Kasturbai (kas-ter-BYE-eye)

Laxmidas (LAX-mi-das)

Maganlal (ma-gan-LAL)

Mahadev Desai (MAY-ha-dev day-SIGH)

Malala Yousafzai
    (mah-LAH-lah YOU-sahf-sigh)

Manilal (MAN-i-lal)

Mendhi (MEH-dee)

Mohandas Karamchand Gandhi
    (MO-han-das kar-UM-chand GAN-dee)

Muhammad Ali Jinnah
    (moo-HAHM-ed AL-ee JIN-nah)

Nan Khatai (naan-ka-TIE)

Nelson Rolihlahla Mandela
    (NEL-sun ho-lee-SHA-sha man-DEL-a)

Putlibai (put-lee-BYE-ah)

Raliatbehn (ra-lee-AT-behn)

Ramdas (RAM-das)

Rangoli (ran-GO-lee)

Tensin Gyatso (TEN-sin CHAI-aht-so)

GLOSSARY

ahimsa (ah-HIM-sa) Compassionate and nonviolent actions, words, and thoughts toward all living things

apartheid (a-PAR-teyt) An unjust government system of South Africa that separated people based on race and skin color

avatar (AV-a-tar) A Hindu god or goddess in human or animal form

Bapu (BA-poo) An affectionate Hindi word for "father"

Bhagavad-Gita (BA-ga-vad GEE-ta) A sacred Hindu text that means "song of God"

brahmacharya (brah-muh-CHAR-ee yuh) Celibacy; a virtuous lifestyle of self-restraint

Buddhism (BOO-diz-em) A major world religion whose followers are called Buddhists; based on the teachings of Buddha

caste (kast) A hierarchical social class in traditional Hindu society

charkha (CHAR-ka) A spinning wheel

Christianity (kris-chee-AN-i-tee) A major world religion whose followers are called Christians; based on the teachings of Jesus Christ

Dalit (DAL-it) A person outside the traditional Hindu caste system; formerly called "untouchable"

deity (DEE-a-tee) A god or goddess

dharma (DAR-ma) The basic nature of the universe and a person's essence; the path of righteousness and joy

Diwali (di-WALL-ee) The Hindu festival of lights celebrated in October and November

Ganesha (ga-NE-shah) The Hindu god of wisdom and remover of life's obstacles

Gujarati (goo-ja-RA-tee) The native language of Gujarat, India

Hind Swaraj (hind swa-RAJ) A book written by Gandhi meaning "Indian Home Rule"

Hindi (HIN-dee) An official language of India

Hinduism (HIN-do-iz-em) A major world religion whose followers are called Hindus; the predominant religion of India

Islam (is-LAHM) A major world religion whose followers are called Muslims; founded by the prophet Muhammad

Jainism (JINE-iz-um) An ancient religion related to, but different from, Hinduism that emphasizes ahimsa

karma (KAR-ma) The positive or negative consequences of one's behavior

khadi (KA-dee) Handwoven cotton cloth produced in India

Krishna (KRISH-nah) The most celebrated Hindu deity, whose life is described in the Bhagavad-Gita; an avatar of Vishnu

Lakshmi (luk-SCHMEE) The Hindu goddess of wealth, fortune, and prosperity

mantra (MAAN-tra) A word repeated in meditation

meditation (med-i-TAY-shun) Concentrated inward focus

om (ohm) A sacred mantra with a mystical sound when chanted

puja (POO-dja) Hindu worship and ritual

Rama (RA-ma) An avatar of Vishnu; the central figure in the Hindu epic, *Ramayana*

reincarnation (re-in-kar-NA-shun) The cycle of birth, life, death, and rebirth; samsara

samsara (sum-SAR-uh) The cycle of birth, life, death, and rebirth; reincarnation

Sanskrit (SAN-skrit) The ancient classic language of India used in Hinduism, Buddhism, and Jainism

Satyagraha (SUT-ee-a-gra-ha) Gandhi's method of nonviolence for social reform

Sikh (seek) A follower of Sikhism, a religion of northern India

Vaishnavism (vay-shna-VISM) A principal denomination of Hinduism, which honors Vishnu as God

Vedas (VAY-duhs) The ancient and sacred scriptures of Hinduism

Vishnu (VEE-shnu) The Supreme God of Vaishnavism

yoga (YO-ga) An ancient form of Indian exercise combining specific body postures, breathing techniques, and meditation

PLACES TO VISIT, IN PERSON OR ONLINE

National Gandhi Museum
New Delhi, India
www.gandhimuseum.org/site
Visitors can explore a variety of galleries and see personal relics of Gandhi, such as manuscripts, journals, and photographs. The museum is at Gandhi's Raj Ghat memorial.

Gandhi Ashram at Sabarmati
Ahmedabad, Gujarat, India
www.gandhiashramsabarmati.org/en
Tour Gandhi's Sabarmati Ashram for a real-life visit to where he and his family lived. A museum at the ashram depicts Gandhi's life from 1915 to 1930. Photographs, artwork, and relics are featured throughout.

Gandhi Memorial Museum, Madurai
Tamil Nadu, India
www.gandhimmm.org
This museum is a global center for training, teaching, and research in peace and conflict studies, Gandhian studies, and yoga.

Kirti Mandir
Porbandar, India
https://en.wikipedia.org/wiki/Kirti_Mandir,_Porbandar
Kirti Mandir is the memorial temple built to honor Mohandas and Kasturba Gandhi in their hometown of Porbandar, India. Visitors will have a chance to visit Gandhi's home, which is adjacent to the memorial, and explore a small museum.

WEBSITES TO EXPLORE

Gandhi Heritage Portal

www.gandhiheritageportal.org

An excellent, comprehensive website about Gandhi that includes biographical information, photographs, videos, writings, journals, books, maps, and much more. Headquartered in Ahmedabad, India, the Gandhi Heritage Portal was founded in 2013 by the Sabarmati Ashram Preservation and Memorial Trust.

M.K. Gandhi Institute for Nonviolence

www.gandhiinstitute.org

This website is a great source for information, resources, educational programs, workshops, videos, and podcasts about achieving nonviolence in the world via learning about Gandhi's life and ideals. The institute is a nonprofit organization founded in 1991 by Gandhi's grandson Arun Gandhi and his wife, Sunanda Gandhi, and is affiliated with the University of Rochester, New York.

Mahatma Gandhi

www.mkgandhi.org

This extensive website offers a wide range of Gandhi's writings, speeches, philosophy, audio, video, and photographs. The website is easy to navigate and has a great deal of interesting and useful information. It is associated with the Bombay Sarvodaya Mandal, Gandhi Book Centre, and Gandhi Research Foundation.

PeaceJam

www.peacejam.org

The PeaceJam Foundation, located in Arvada, Colorado, is an international education program focused on working with young people to promote peace around the world.

The Metta Center for Nonviolence

mettacenter.org

An organization in Petaluma, California, dedicated to promoting an understanding of nonviolence and peace in our world.

The Ahimsa Center

www.cpp.edu/~ahimsacenter/ahimsa_home.shtml

This center was established in 2004 at California State Polytechnic University in Pomona, California. The center focuses on the positive influences of nonviolence and ahimsa in our world today.

NOTES

INTRODUCTION

"Generations to come": Alice Calaprice, ed., *The New Quotable Einstein* (Princeton, NJ: Princeton University Press, 2005), 80.

CHAPTER 1

"If we coud change": M. K. Gandhi, *The Collected Works of Mahatma Gandhi*, Vol. 12, 158.

"My father": M. K. Gandhi, *Gandhi: An Autobiography; The Story of My Experiments with Truth*, 3.

"To keep two or three": M. K. Gandhi, *Autobiography*, 5.

CHAPTER 2

"If a man": Henry David Thoreau, *Walden* (New York: Library of America Paperback Classics, 2010), 261.

"There is hardly anything": M. K. Gandhi, *Gandhi: An Autobiography; The Story of My Experiments with Truth*, 6.

"I do not think": M. K. Gandhi, *Autobiography*, 9.

"Everything on that day": M. K. Gandhi, *Autobiography*, 10.

"two innocent children": M. K. Gandhi, *Autobiography*, 11.

"poor mite": M. K. Gandhi, *Autobiography*, 31.

"I went": M. K. Gandhi, *Autobiography*, 35.

"One dark night": M. K. Gandhi, *London Diary, The Collected Works of Mahatma Gandhi*, Vol. 1, 10.

"From the date": M. K. Gandhi, *London Diary*, 48.

CHAPTER 3

"The only tired": Rosa Parks, with Jim Haskins, *Rosa Parks: My Story* (New York: Puffin Books, 1992), 116.

"My grief": M. K. Gandhi, *Gandhi: An Autobiography; The Story of My Experiments with Truth*, 87.

"The storm": M. K. Gandhi, *Autobiography*, 90.

"I did not like": M. K. Gandhi, *Autobiography*, 90.

"We had long": M. K. Gandhi, *Autobiography*, 106.

"unwelcome visitor": M. K. Gandhi, *Autobiography*, 108.

"deep disease": M. K. Gandhi, *Autobiography*, 112.

"My speech": M. K. Gandhi, *Autobiography*, 126.

"Gandhi!": M. K. Gandhi, *Autobiography*, 192.

"Mohandas had seen": Arun Gandhi, *Kasturba: A Life*, 92.

CHAPTER 4

"No scene": John Ruskin, *Unto This Last* (Minneapolis: Filiquarian, 2007), 95.

"I determined to change": M. K. Gandhi, *Gandhi: An Autobiography; The Story of My Experiments with Truth*, 298.

"wild, snake-infested outpost": Arun Gandhi, *Kasturba: A Life*, 132.

"man-hunt": M. K. Gandhi, *Autobiography*, 315.

"from their gestures": M. K. Gandhi, *Satyagraha in South Africa*, 154.

"The Zulus were delighted": M. K. Gandhi, *Autobiography*, 314.

"She had no objection": M. K. Gandhi, *Autobiography*, 208.

"No more work": M. K. Gandhi, *Satyagraha*, 364.

"It follows": M. K. Gandhi, *Key to Health*, 79.

"The inner working": M. K. Gandhi, *Key to Health*, 5.

"do as their heads": M. K. Gandhi, *Key to Health*, 53.

CHAPTER 5

"Peace is available": Thich Nhat Hahn, *Peace Is Every Step: The Path of Mindfulness in Everyday Life* (New York: Bantam Books, 1992), 134.

"all laws": M. K. Gandhi, *Satyagraha in South Africa*, 136.

"I shuddered": M. K. Gandhi, *Satyagraha*, 155.

"We might have to": M. K. Gandhi, *Satyagraha*, 167.

"Those who have committed": M. K. Gandhi, *Satyagraha*, 261.

"By burning the certificates": M. K. Gandhi, *Satyagraha*, 312.

"On the one hand": M. K. Gandhi, *Satyagraha*, 355.

"The pilgrim band": M. K. Gandhi, *Satyagraha*, 456.

"it was a great wrench": M. K. Gandhi, *Satyagraha*, 509.

CHAPTER 6

"Gandhi did not": Scott London, "In the Footsteps of Gandhi: An Interview with Vandana Shiva," from the public radio series *Insight and Outlook*, 1998, www.scottlondon.com/interviews/shiva.html.

"I felt that Indians": M. K. Gandhi, *Gandhi: An Autobiography; The Story of My Experiments with Truth*, 346.

"Great Soul": Fischer, *Gandhi: His Life and Message for the World*, 55.

"The ryots": M. K. Gandhi, *Autobiography*, 425.

"India's problems": Arun Gandhi, *Kasturba: A Life*, 208.

"It was unbearable": M. K. Gandhi, *Autobiography*, 468.

"non-co-operation": M.K. Gandhi, *Autobiography*, 481.

"The object that we set": M. K. Gandhi, *Autobiography*, 489.

CHAPTER 7

"To think": Arun Gandhi, *Kasturba: A Life*, 244.

"The volunteers": Webb Miller, "Natives Beaten Down by Police in India Salt Bed Raid," United Press International, May 21, 1930.

"The British were deeply embarrassed": Furbee and Furbee, *The Importance of Mohandas Gandhi*, 74.

"frantic negotiations": Bush, *Mohandas Gandhi*, 75.

"strong critic of Nazi Germany": "Mohandas K. Gandhi: The Indian Leader at Home and Abroad," obituary, *New York Times*, January 31, 1948.

"It is quite clear": M. K. Gandhi, *The Collected Works of Mahatma Gandhi*, Vol. 70, 20.

"What did you enjoy": Ellen Mahoney phone interview with Arun Gandhi, October 2014.

"The light that has": Jack, *The Gandhi Reader*, 488.

CHAPTER 8

"This is what": Malala Yousafzai, Speech to the United Nations, July 12, 2013, A World at School, transcript of speech, https://secure.aworldatschool.org/page/content/the-text-of-malala-yousafzais-speech-at-the-united-nations/.

"While the Montgomery boycott": King, "My Trip to the Land of Gandhi," 84.

"I accept it": The 14th Dalai Lama, Nobel Peace Prize 1989 acceptance speech, www.dalailama.com/messages/acceptance-speeches/nobel-peace-prize.

BIBLIOGRAPHY

* *Titles suited for younger readers*

*Bush, Catherine. *Mohandas Gandhi*. London: Burke, 1988.

*Chatterjee, Manini, and Anita Roy. *India*. New York: Dorling Kindersley, 2002.

*Desai, Narayan. *Gandhi Through a Child's Eyes: An Intimate Memoir*. Santa Fe, NM: Ocean Tree Books, 1992.

Desai, Narayan, and Tridip Suhrud. *My Life Is My Message*. 4 vols. New Delhi, India: Orient BlackSwan, 2009.

Fischer, Louis. *Gandhi: His Life and Message for the World*. New York: Signet Classics, 2010.

*Furbee, Mary, and Mike Furbee. *The Importance of Mohandas Gandhi*. San Diego: Lucent Books, 2000.

Gandhi, Arun. *Kasturba: A Life*. New Delhi, India: Penguin Books India, 2000.

*Gandhi, Arun. *Legacy of Love: My Education in the Path of Nonviolence*. El Sobrante, CA: North Bay Books, 2003.

*Gandhi, Arun, and Bethany Hegedus. *Grandfather Gandhi*. New York: Atheneum Books for Young Readers, 2014.

Gandhi, M. K. *The Collected Works of Mahatma Gandhi*. Vol. 1, 1884–1896, Vol. 12, 1913–1914, and Vol. 70, 1939. New Delhi, India: Navajivan Trust, 1977. Gandhi Heritage Portal. www.gandhi heritageportal.org/the-collected-works-of-mahatma-gandhi.

Gandhi, M. K. *Gandhi: An Autobiography; The Story of My Experiments with Truth*. Boston: Beacon Press, 1993.

Gandhi, M. K. *Key to Health*. Ahmedabad, India: Navajivan Press, 1948. Gandhi Heritage Portal. www.gandhiheritageportal.org /mahatma-gandhi-books/key-to-health#page/1/mode/2up.

Gandhi, M. K. *Satyagraha in South Africa*. Madras, India: S. Ganesan, 1928. Gandhi Heritage Portal. www.gandhiheritageportal.org /mahatma-gandhi-books/satyagraha-in-south-africa#page/1 /mode/2up.

Jack, Homer A. *The Gandhi Reader: A Sourcebook of His Life and Writings*. New York: Grove Press, 1994.

Jones, E. Stanley. *Gandhi: Portrayal of a Friend*. Nashville: Abingdon Classics, 1993.

King, Martin Luther, Jr. "My Trip to the Land of Gandhi." *Ebony*, July 1959.

Miller, Barbara S., trans. *The Bhagavad-Gita: Krishna's Counsel in Time of War*. New York: Bantam Dell, 2004.

*Pastan, Amy. *Gandhi: A Photographic Story of a Life*. New York: DK, 2006.

*Patel, Sanjay. *The Little Book of Hindu Deities*. New York: Plume, 2006.

*Saklani, Juhi. *Eyewitness Gandhi*. London: Dorling Kindersley, 2014.

*Todd, Anne M. *Mohandas Gandhi*. Philadelphia: Chelsea House, 2004.

*Wilkinson, Philip. *Gandhi: The Young Protester Who Founded a Nation*. Washington, DC: National Geographic Society, 2007.

INDEX